To order, call 1-800-765-6955.

Visit our Web site at *www.reviewandherald.com* for information on other Review and Herald products.

The author's e-mail address is: *LorettaSpivey7@aol.com* .

straight talk

SEX

Loretta Parker Spivey

**How Teens Can
Make Wise Choices
About Love and Sex**

REVIEW AND HERALD® PUBLISHING ASSOCIATION
HAGERSTOWN, MD 21740

The author assumes full responsibility for the accuracy of all facts
and quotations as cited in this book.

Texts credited to Clear Word are from *The Clear Word,* copyright © 1994 by Jack J. Blanco.
Texts credited to NKJV are from the New King James Version. Copyright © 1979, 1980, 1982 by Thomas Nelson, Inc. Used by permission. All rights reserved.

This book was
Edited by Gerald Wheeler
Designed by Willie Duke
Electronic makeup by Shirley M. Bolivar
Cover designed by Edgerton.• Bond Image Design/Mark Bond
Typeset: 11/14 Veljovic Book

PRINTED IN U.S.A.

04 03 02 01   5 4 3 2

R&H Cataloging Service
Spivey, Loretta Parker
   Straight talk.
      1. Sexual abstinence.   I. Title
                176

ISBN 0-8280-1443-4

Dedication

Father, in Jesus' name I dedicate this book to You. Please bless each person who searches for the truth in its pages. Show them the truth about You. You are faithful! You are forgiving! You are awesome! I love You, Lord.

Words of Thanks

Mom: I love you! Thanks for your never-ending support.

Wyatt: What do St. Francis Hospital, surgery, this book, and you have in common? Thanks for your help in trying to find a title (smiles).

Darryl: (Did I mention that you are the best, most handsome, most patient husband a girl can have?) I need a whole book to tell the story of your love and support. You are a godsend. I love you!

"The Group" at Hope Seventh-day Adventist Church: For reading and reading and reading . . . thank you for your input and support and for allowing me to be a part of your lives.

Gina, Linda, Lisa (LLL & G nope forever), Rena (to the max!), Alease, and Ms. Moore (I am regressing). When I could not type another word, when I wanted to give up, when (well, you know the details) you prayed and encouraged and prayed some more. Thanks so much!

The participants: For the tears shed as you remembered, for the embarrassment you felt as you shared, for pressing through the really hard parts of the interview, and for trusting me with your heart and your story, I am ever indebted to you. Literally, this book would not exist without you. I can't even thank you by name because I need to protect you, but know that I love you and thank my God for every remembrance of you. Thanks for making a difference.

Contents

Introduction

"Hey, Rette. Did you ever 'do it'?" The question was simple, yet it was also extremely complex. It was a short question that required a long answer. Imbedded in the question was the desire for honest dialog about sex. It had all the legitimate curiosity of a teenager and the need for much more information than I, a 20something virgin struggling to stay that way, was able to give at the moment.

But somehow I knew that the question with all its inherent and unspoken messages must be addressed, and that is the purpose of this book. Through the experiences of real people we will take an honest look at the issue of premarital sex. The stories are true, although I have changed the names and places to protect the identity of those who so unselfishly shared their stories. I know that God will speak through them to you. Please open your heart. He has a special message just for you.

Dear Parent:

Please, please talk to your young people about sex. They face serious attack from the enemy of souls, and if you don't take the time and energy to tell them the truth, Satan will provide some perverted TV show, movie, video, song, magazine, or—God forbid—relative to give information—or worse yet—experience to your child. I encourage you to use the stories here as a springboard for discussion. Other books are available as well. Employ as many resources as you wish, but please tell your children. If you don't, Satan will!

—Loretta Parker Spivey

Together Forever . . . Unfortunately

June's Story

Is your father missing from your life?
Do you find yourself looking for love in all the wrong places?
Do you need to hear the words "I love you"?
Have you messed up and feel that you need big-time forgiveness?
One yes answer means that you and June have something in common.
This may be the chapter that is just for you.

Single-parent home
Three younger siblings
Raised by grandparents
They forced me to abort my baby!

My grandmother called my mother, and they made the decision. I had no say whatsoever. I wasn't happy about it; even though I was only 14 I wanted my baby—if I had kept it maybe Pete would have grown to love me again. There was a time that he loved me. He said that was why we had sex in the first place.

I was baby-sitting, and Pete came by the house to keep me company. "June, I love you," he said. Not only did he tell me; he showed me. Earlier he had given me a really nice engraved bracelet. I was 14 years old, and it was literally the first time I had heard a male tell me that he loved me. It sounded good, and I believed him. Pete showed up that night with a plan and I cooperated fully, even though I knew nothing of what he had in mind. I just knew that we loved each other.

The next month when I didn't have a period I really didn't pay attention to it. The month after that I still didn't have a period, and again I didn't worry. I was naive. Meanwhile, I decided that since I was going to be having sex, I needed to get some birth control pills. Pete and I had had sex 2 or 3 times up to that point. My girl-friend and I went to the hospital to get birth control pills. The nurse said to us, "OK, you girls want to get on the pill; your parents don't have to know. But before we do this we need to take a pregnancy test."

The nurse came back and told me I was pregnant. I had been feeling a little funny and hurting a little bit so I asked, "Could it be that something is wrong with my gall bladder? Or could it be . . . ?" I tried to blame it on everything else—except me having sex.

When the nurse finally convinced me that I was preg-nant, I cried. She asked me what I wanted to do, then told me I had some decisions to make. I was so confused. But I knew that because I loved Pete and he loved me I wanted to keep my baby. After all, he had told me he loved me and had bought me the bracelet. He loved me, and I wanted to have his baby. I must say that he showed his love in a strange way, though. When I told him that I was pregnant, he was kind of nonchalant about it. It was like "Whatever, I ain't gonna marry you." Then he started being cold and distant.

When I was 12 my grandmother had taken me home with her in an attempt to rescue me from the "evils" of living with my mother. But by then I had already seen a lot. A single parent, my mom had had me when she was about 17. I have four brothers and sisters, and together we have three different fathers. My mother and father never married. However, my father ended up marrying my mother's second cousin. So I have cousins who are also my half sisters. My mother was not ready to really be a mom, so she was kind of wild. Although raised in the church, she was into parties and the fast life. My mom's house was the local hangout.

But even then I did not know very much. My mother never said anything to me about sex, and my grandmother told me that if I kissed a boy I was going to get pregnant. It wasn't until my older cousin moved into my grandma's house that I learned the real deal. She started schooling me on the topic. Shortly after she moved into town we started hanging out with guys (I was too young for boyfriends, but she wasn't). My cousin told me that I should have sex with Pete.

Anyway, my grandmother found out that I was pregnant. She took me to get a pregnancy test, and of course it came back positive. I was 14 years old, pregnant, in love, and forced to abort my baby. All I could think was that it's not supposed to be like this.

OK, you have the circumstances. Now, I want to tell a bit about myself. I had very low self-esteem, because I was extremely skinny. In fact, I had a complex about being so thin. People often told me that I could never do anything right and that I would never become anything or anybody. They said I was skinny and ugly. So you can see why I was so excited when an older (he was 17), popular guy showed some interest in me and told me that he loved me.

Unfortunately, there was not one positive male in my life. Well, I take that back. My grandfather was there, and he was still married to my grandmother after many years. He worked hard and took care of us and gave us money when we needed it, but he never told me, "June, I love you," even though I guess I knew that he did in his own quiet way. So, there I was, craving attention from a man.

In all honesty I was probably longing for attention from my father, who wanted nothing to do with me, so I turned to a 17-year-old boy who knew nothing about real love.

I wish I had known then what I do now, but nobody told me. I did not know that God loved me and that He created me to have sex with *one* man, my husband. Nobody explained to me how important it is to save yourself for your husband. Nobody ever told me that I was a jewel or explained the importance of waiting until I was married. They said, "Don't do it," but nobody bothered to say why. They didn't help me to see that sex creates a covenant. That it is a soul tie in the sense that you are bonding with the other person, taking on his or her character. But nobody ever pointed that out to me.

When I gave myself to Pete I thought that I was in love. He was a part of me now, we were as one. That is what I felt. It is always a deeper emotional experience for women than it is for men. The next day, though, he was cool, and I didn't hear the "I love yous." Instead, he seemed to feel that I was now his "woman," so he could do what he wanted. I did not understand what was going on. His behavior hurt me. I did not get support from him, especially after the abortion. But I kept going back to him. We continued to see each other and to have sex.

Mind you, we had no relationship other than that at that time. We called it "messin' around" in those days. He would say, "She's not my girlfriend; we're just messin'." Of course, I was on the pill by then and considered myself protected. And I was, but only from pregnancy. Not from sexually transmitted diseases and certainly not from the emotional scars that accompany sex outside of the bond of marriage.

Pete eventually got a friend of mine pregnant. His was her second child. She had the baby and he stuck with her, but used to flirt with me just to keep me close. Finally, I sensed it was time to move on. But I did not realize that sex was not the way to gain the love and affection of a real man.

By this time I was 16 or 17 and had met a college guy. He was cute, a basketball player, and he liked me. One day he and I were walking around downtown at some type of fair or expo, just enjoying the sights. It was all pretty innocent at that time. Later I visited a friend, who happened to be Pete's cousin. Pete came in and demanded, "What were you doing with him [the college guy]? Trying to embarrass me?" Then Pete started trying to hit me.

His father happened to be in the living room. I said, "Mr. Neps, go get your black suit because I am about to kill your son." Going to the kitchen, I found a big butcher knife. Pushing Pete against the wall, I put the knife to his chest and told him that if he ever hit me I would kill him. As I look back I now realize that I was tied to Pete in a way that I really did not understand. Sex had created a bond with him, a bond that was almost impossible to break.

But I continued to think that all the protection I needed was birth control until I became converted in the early 1980s. It all started with a gospel music concert. The music was nice, the words were awesome, and they made me think. Afterward we had an opportunity to meet the singers. They were the nicest guys imaginable, and at first I thought that something was wrong with them, because they were not checking us out. They were complete gentlemen. We had a nice conversation as they talked about God's love. As they ministered to me, they simplified the Word of God in a way that I could really understand. One of them said to me, "You can make God Lord of your life right now. Right now you can become converted."

I kept replying, "Not now, I got these tickets to a secular concert. Maybe after the concert." Later I attended the other concert, got high, then went to my boyfriend's place and had sex afterward, but it just didn't feel right. I knew that something had changed in my life. The Holy Spirit was working on me.

I started growing spiritually, was faithfully attending church, and consistently studied the Word of God. I was cleaning up my vocabulary and getting away from the drugs, but it was not very easy to conquer the sex thing.

I felt really condemned for doing it, but that didn't stop me. At that time I had a boyfriend who was a Muslim, and I felt that I had to break off our relationship gradually. I had sex with him and even smoked a couple joints, but it didn't feel right. It wasn't as much fun. I knew it was wrong and that I wanted to grow in Christ. I really wanted to be a committed Christian. The Muslim and I eventually broke up.

The next guy I liked was cute, smart, and had a great personality. Besides, he was a college student and a Christian. The first thing I thought was that he would never like me. I still struggled with poor self-esteem and was plagued by a string of bad relationships. He did like me, though, and we became very good friends.

One night we were talking at the kitchen table and next thing I knew we were in the family room on the floor, intensely making out. We didn't have intercourse, because we were both afraid since I was not on any form of birth control. You know what? It was still fornication. True, there was no intercourse, but we were still having sex. It was wrong, and we both knew it. Although I was in love again, I realized that it wasn't going to work out, that he would choose a college-educated girl over me. Well, after all kinds of craziness, including him doing a disappearing act for a few weeks, he did finally marry someone else. Once again I was heartbroken.

The incident with the college man left me really discouraged. Discouraged with bad relationships, discouraged with my walk with God. It was a down period in my life. And I was also backsliding, doing things (other than sex) that I should not have been doing. Right in the midst of my depression along came Jay. He was nice, but I just didn't want to be bothered at the time. When he asked for my phone number, I wouldn't give it to him, so he obtained it from a mutual friend. Jay was quite determined. We had sex on our second date, and I got pregnant again. It was horrible, because I had not been sexually active for a while (except for that close call with the college guy) and Jay just caught me at a weak point in my life. When I told him that I was pregnant, he replied, "I can't deal with this. I just had a baby three months ago."

"OK, fine, but I'm not killing this baby," I told him. "Nobody is going to make me abort this one. You know what, Jay, I will take care of my own baby. I don't need you to buy Pampers, milk, nothing. You will never even see this baby."

I had not yet told my family that I was pregnant. After their reaction to my first pregnancy and Jay's response, I was not sure what to expect. This time, however, my grandmother announced, "We are going to take care of this baby." She also told me to make sure that I got child support from Jay. My other family members were also ready to chip in and help.

My pastor called me unexpectedly one night and asked me what was wrong. Through bitter tears I told him that I was pregnant. Both he and his wife promised to help me. I was glad for all the support—I needed it.

Besides going through pressure at work and struggling with some spiritual issues, now I was pregnant again, and the father was too occupied with his other children (I found out he actually had *two* additional children). I was depressed to the point that I was ready to kill myself. To make matters worse, the pregnancy left me really sick. I was always either spotting or throwing up. One day I began hemorrhaging. When I went to the hospital I learned that I had actually miscarried at home. I remembered a big glob of something falling into the toilet (I had thought maybe it was a big blood clot). My depression worsened after I lost the baby. Everybody said they loved me, but I felt like nobody really did.

I can't explain what happened next. When you have never had the love of a real man in your life, it is easy to be gullible. And I guess that is what happened. Since the previous relationship hadn't worked out, I told myself, maybe the next one would. When it failed, I again thought, *Maybe this one will.* Looking for love in all the wrong places, I got so disgusted that I hated my life. And I had to get away.

In desperation I moved out of state to seek a fresh start. It took a while, but I found a job and an apartment and located a good church where I met lots of nice single people. As I kept myself busy with positive activities, things began looking up.

At last I was on the right track. Then after about a year or two of no sex I got involved with a guy who was not converted. He attended church, but he just went to sharpen his musical skills, because his plan was to become a secular musician. Unfortunately, I fell back into the same mind-set. "This man really loves me. Maybe I can work on his relationship with God." Don't be deceived. It doesn't work. You can't change a person through your own efforts. Fortunately, that relationship didn't last long. God was really working with me, and I was becoming more and more committed to Him.

Finally I decided that I was not getting married but was going to give my life completely to God. I was tired of bad relationship after bad relationship. It was just too hard, and I didn't want to be hurt or to disappoint God again. Mentally and physically it wasn't worth the resulting pain. Every single man in my life had been a disappointment, and I had given my all in almost every case. At last I had learned a very important lesson.

I discovered that when you sleep with someone, that person's personality enters you. It is like a "soul tie." You are bonded to each other for life. And those ties will come back to haunt you in your future. That is why I felt so messed up and depressed.

Also I found out the hard way that all those men shared a very private and sacred part of me. I wish someone had taken the time to tell me how I was as a woman and how sacred my virginity was and that it is not something to share with just anybody. Maybe then I wouldn't have been so quick to sleep with the first boy who told me he loved me and bought me a little cheap bracelet.

Guilt and the need for forgiveness are big consequences of having sex outside of the marriage bond. First of all, I had to suffer the consequences of being religious and feeling guilty all at the same time. Of feeling as if I wasn't worthy to serve God or be used by Him. That was hard, because I knew that God had something special for me to do for Him even back then. I kept asking myself, "How could God possibly do anything through me? I have messed up too many times."

Satan knew he could really overwhelm me with guilt. He tried to take away my sense of purpose, kill my dreams, and have me walk away defeated. You have to get to a point at which you say, "Lord, no matter what, if I fall again I am going to get up and keep going, but I am sticking with You and am accepting Your forgiveness." It is a hard thing to do, because you have to grow into that kind of relationship. You have to let the past be the past.

I used to scold myself, "Lord, I really blew it. I can't ever get my virginity back." But then I started growing more and saying to myself, "Lord, I am a new creature in You." As I read the Word, a healing process took place. Physically, I might not be a virgin, but I had dedicated my life to God and given my body back to Him. And God, being the loving, forgiving Lord that He is, took me back and made me whole again.

What happened? The Lord brought the man who would eventually become my husband into my life. Isn't that just like Him? As soon as I learned the lessons He wanted me to acquire, as soon as I stopped looking for love from worthless men and started looking to Him, He gave me a wonderful man of God. A perfect gentleman in every way. God worked it out as only He could. Our relationship was not about the physical. Our conversations were about our dreams and aspirations.

Quickly we discovered that we liked the same things. Both of us loved God. He would minister to me and I would minister to him, and we prayed for each other.

When we married I breathed a sigh of relief. The battle was over, and with God's help I was the victor (or so I thought).

But I had one more battle to fight—I had to deal with all the baggage from all my other relationships. Yes, I had forgiven myself. Yes, God had forgiven me, but the other men were still there. I carried all those other people into my marriage. I had to let go completely of those other men I was still bonded to. Only the power of God released and freed me. You have to allow the love of God and His Word to cleanse you from all other relationships.

Yes, God ultimately gave me a good, Christian man, and I felt pure because I never slept with my husband before we were married, and it was worth the wait. I thank God for that. And I am proud of that! We have been married eight years now.

Even though my story has a great ending, I encourage you to look at the whole story. I went through stress, depression, and confusion, not to mention an abortion and a miscarriage, all because I was disobedient. I can't stress how dangerous it is to connect sexually with someone other than the person to whom you are married.

My last words are simple ones: Don't do it. Don't have sex until you walk down that aisle, until after the two of you have made a commitment before God and the people. I don't care if you are in love and engaged, until you both declare "I do," you must first say, "I don't and I won't!"

It Just Happened 2

Planning to get married "just because" you are pregnant?
Planning to marry a non-Christian and change him or her?
Have you ever said, "We don't plan to have sex; it just happens"?
Do you think that birth control is the answer to the consequences of
*   premarital sex?*
If you answered yes to any of the above questions, this chapter is for you.

Female
Raised in a Christian home by grandmother
Never really thought about sex until it happened

The funny thing is that I don't really recall making a conscious decision to have sex. As I look back, I am sure that my childhood had a lot to do with the decisions that I made. I was raised in a conservative home by my grandmother. My dad was there until I was about 12. For the most part his alcoholic lifestyle kept him apart from us. The more I think about it, I really don't ever recall making a conscious decision to engage in premarital sex. It just happened, and I didn't stop it.

I do remember being confused. It is as if, somehow deep in your heart, you know you don't want to do it, but another part of you feels compelled to go through with it. I can hear Aunt Frances now. She says, "Your mind is saying no! but your body is screaming y-e-s!" And she is right. The combination of all those new tingly feelings and the lack of clear thinking about what could happen long-term dulls your ability to be strong in such moments. Plus, a lot of social and environmental factors played out in our relationship.

I was the oldest in my family. Dave was the youngest in his. My childhood was burdensome and harsh. Dave suffered much rejection from his older siblings. Our friendship brought with it so much baggage that neither of us was aware of how we were doomed to fail from the very beginning. Throughout the course of our relationship we fought the world together to keep our sanity. It was like a made-for-TV movie—two young people in love, standing against the world and our dysfunctional families. That dynamic just drew us closer together.

Sex, for him, was a form of acceptance. I just seemed to let it happen, because it was not as unpleasant as so much of my life was. I think that is where most young people get caught. They don't understand the perceived need in their lives for sex. Looking back, I see that rejection played a larger part in my decision to have sex than I realized. In fact, it probably has a major role in most young people's decisions to have sex. Dave and I didn't say to each other, "We're feeling lonely and rejected, so let's have sex and make each other feel accepted." Instead, it just happened, and once you experience sex and seem to get away with it, you want to keep doing it. It's kind of funny that we think of pregnancy as the only consequence of premarital sex, that if you don't get pregnant or caught naked by your parents, then you got away with it!

Anyway, since we didn't get caught, we looked for chances to do it again. We didn't openly seek out ways to be alone and have sex. We just seemed to ease into situations that would allow us to be alone together.

Neither of us consciously said, "We're going to have sex today." It just happened.

We did take advantage of our circumstances, though. I remember I was baby-sitting for a neighbor one evening. For some reason the mother of the children also sent Dave to the house. The kids were already in bed, and we discovered (but never said out loud) that there was really nothing keeping us from having sex. As we danced together one thing led to another. We had no respect for the person's home or the sleeping kids. Of course, sex was not on our minds at all in the beginning. It was something that we just let happen. Afterward, it was our little secret, and it drew us closer together. Somehow it is kind of funny because, at any given moment that evening, we both thought that we would stop; we thought we might get caught. But we continued with the dancing and the kissing until we did it right there in the neighbor's house.

Having sex with Dave was fairly easy on the conscience because we never planned it. Like I said, we just ended up in places that left us alone, and one thing always led to another. We just ended up doing it. It was never planned.

Even now I can still feel my horror when I learned I was pregnant. I was 16, and the pressure was horrible. I really don't even have the words to describe it. Believe me when I tell you that premarital sex and resulting pregnancy lead to pre-everything. Preadulthood. Premotherhood. Preschool preparation for your child when you should be making your own college plans. Pregrown-up problems. My childhood passed me by. Friends often grow up and grow apart, but my friendships were cut short prematurely because "good girls" didn't associate with "bad girls" like me even though these girls were also sexually active and just hadn't gotten pregnant yet.

There was also a tremendous strain on my relationship with Dave. We faced major financial burdens. Who would care for my baby financially? To make matters worse, my mom was on public assistance at the time, and her caseworker said that my pregnancy would cause her checks to be cut. The rule was that we would have to get financial support from the father of the child. Dave didn't work except at a car wash, where he made pennies compared to what we needed. Talk about growing up fast. My youth disappeared overnight.

I wish someone had taken the time to tell me how special I was and that I should expect boys to respect me and think of me as a special creation of God. I wish that someone had warned me about the sexual feelings that I would experience. I wish that someone had explained to me that teenagers have all kinds of sexual feelings that are not abnormal, but that need to be controlled. Those chills and tinglings feel like love to an unaware teenager. Experiencing them for the first time makes you feel so wonderful and alive and so loved that you desperately want to believe that this is the person for you and that sex is the way you need to express your emotions. The saying "to be forewarned is to be forearmed" is true. I was not warned, and therefore was not armed. I was unprepared for the battle.

Being forewarned also helps you to discover more about yourself and how you process and deal with the environmental influences and emotional baggage that can negatively influence your decision-making process in many areas of life.

When I got pregnant my mother was just in her early

30s and not at all happy about becoming a grandmother, so she set out to make Dave's and my life miserable. Dave and I didn't know how to handle the pressure, so we stopped seeing each other. So there I was 16, pregnant, my mother angry at me, an absent alcoholic father, and no boyfriend. Not a good place to be.

Eventually we did get back together. And interestingly enough we were not sexually active for a long time. It was almost as if we had learned our lesson, even though we didn't talk about it. Eventually, he began to push for intimacy again. Looking back, it seems rather strange to me that even during the second time around in our relationship we didn't plan to have sex. It just happened. Once again we just ended up in places that were convenient. Even after our first child and a long separation we never really set out to have sex.

This time around, though, we got married. We felt that it was the right thing to do. Besides, I was pregnant with our second child. I wish I had known more about life, more about dating, more about myself, more about how important school and my future were, more about careers—more about life in general.

So, there we were—teenagers married with two children. Yet I kept thinking and hoping that I was finally getting on track. At least I was married and things would approach some degree of normalcy. But life can't be normal for teenagers who are married with children. It is as if you desperately need food and you get some, but you can't eat it. Instead, you have to give it away. We were kids, needing love, support, and nurturing from our parents, but instead we were expected to be giving it to our children. In addition, we had very poor examples of what a family was really supposed to act like.

As we were trying to meet our financial obligations, take care of our two children, and just make it through this tough time, along came child number three. If someone were telling me my own story, my first question would be why I didn't use birth control. In those days I was not aware of birth control. That was another taboo subject in my household. I didn't learn about it until after my third child.

Yet in a way I'm glad that I didn't know about birth control because birth control wasn't the solution for Dave and me. Self-control was the answer. Teens will have sexual feelings and temptations. The issue isn't birth control, but self-control.

Two wrongs don't make a right. One mistake (pregnancy) shouldn't be followed by another mistake (marriage to the wrong person). Too many teens view the unequally yoked concept as a sort of baseball bat that adults use to keep them away from connecting or uniting with others not of their same religion. However, I have learned the hard way that it is much deeper than that, and I really wish that someone had explored the topic with me during my preteen and teenage years. When Dave and I married, people said that dark clouds hang over such relationships. I was raised in the church and attended consistently. But by church standards Dave was "worldly."

It doesn't matter how many other things you have in common if you don't share a common faith, nor does it work if the person comes to Christ just because of the relationship. Going into an "unequally yoked" marriage is just not worth it. God said in 2 Corinthians 6:14: "Don't go into partnership with those who believe dif-

ferently from you. It won't work. How can right have
fellowship with wrong? What does light have in common with darkness?" (Clear Word). He knew what He
was talking about! Not only are Dave and I unequally
yoked from a biblical perspective, we are unequally
yoked in the area of our goals. If I would have taken just
a little time to look into the future, I would have seen
that I had so much more to offer in a relationship and
needed so much more from a relationship than my husband can accept or give.

And if I had married someone who knew how to set
realistic goals, who had some idea of what kind of future
he wanted, who had a plan of some kind for himself, we
could at this point in life be in pursuit of our common
goals. I have discovered that I must find happiness in
other areas of life outside of my marriage so that my life
is not a total waste.

Generally young people don't think about the
future. But they should. They should contemplate the
long-term results that can occur from a short-term Y-E-S!

I Know for Sure I Wanna Wait . . . I Think

Princess's Story

Female
22 years old
Originally from Northeast
Raised as a Christian
Planned to remain a virgin until marriage

It was New Years Day, and we had been in church literally all night. In the morning, after breakfast, we went to catch some zzzzs at a friend's house. The friend was out of town. I can't remember if we discussed that fact or not, but I don't think so. I just know that we fell into bed together. Just a quick Happy New Year peck on the cheek . . . then the lips . . . then the neck. Before I knew it I was in much too deep. It all led to much more than I was able to handle. It was sexy (I had aroused him to the ultimate point), but it was also scary. Even though we never really had intercourse, it was a very close call. Close enough for his sperm to be all over me. Yuck. What if . . . ?

In my inexperience I thought that he should have been able to control himself or at least warn me beforehand. The whole incident was more than I could take. Even mentioning it now makes me cringe. I jumped up and made him get up too, then we put the sheets in the washing machine, showered, and got dressed (all in silence). We never discussed it. There wasn't much to say. We both knew that we had almost really blown it and had come dangerously close to making the mistake of a lifetime.

Dear Loretta,

How are you doing? I am OK, enjoying college life, especially winter break. Just think, I am almost a sophomore. The other kids are nice, and being on a Christian campus is pretty cool. But I have a problem. Promise to keep this between us, OK?

I have been dating this guy since the summer before my freshman year. We met at the youth retreat and just hit it off. We are in love. I mean, really in love. We pray together and go to church together and have many of the same friends. Our relationship is very special, and we believe it is God's will for us to be together. After almost two years together, well—we almost had sex the other night. It wasn't planned or anything. We just ended up alone at a friend's apartment, and one thing led to another. I almost gave in, but at the last minute said no. Actually (this is really embarrassing), he "came" and I got really scared, so I stopped him.

He said that he was glad that I did, but that he loves me and wants to express his love for me. It was wonderful and scary all at the same time. I mean, I know that we should not have sex, but why? Didn't God give us those feelings? Isn't sex for people who love and care about each other? We love each other and are responsible adults. Please tell me what you think—and fast. I am so confused.

Dear Princess,

Thanks for trusting me. I just want to tell you a few things that I hope will help you to understand where you are and how to handle this situation. First of all, this is a spiritual battle. You are struggling against Satan himself, and he will not miss even one opportunity to destroy a commitment to God and His ideal for His children. Satan hates relationships patterned after truth. And he has, from the days of Adam and Eve, sought to destroy pure, Christ-centered relationships. This is a spiritual battle, and you must fight it as such!

What you and Jay are experiencing is natural. Sex is a very beautiful expression of love and oneness. But, and there is really no other way to say it, sex is for married people—period. "God created sex . . . In an environment of love and commitment, there can be no more powerful expression of exclusive intimacy than sex" (*Purity Under Pressure,* p. 75). It is the ultimate gift that two people can give to each other. For a moment two people literally become one. And every time you have sex you leave a part of yourself with that person. Be careful, or by the time you get married you will just be a shell of a person to share with your life mate.

It might feel right and good, but life isn't based on feelings. It is based on love. Love for God. And that is much more than a feeling. Jesus felt distressed, sorrowful, troubled, and overwhelmed as He prayed in the Garden of Gethsemane. He actually said, "I'm so weak, I feel like I'm dying" (Matt. 26:38, Clear Word). Don't believe for one moment that Jesus felt like dying the death of a common criminal on the cross. Think about it—no, take a moment to picture it. Jesus was naked, being smacked around, spit on, called names, and then had a crown of thorns thrust on His head in mockery. Go outside and squeeze the stem of a rose as hard as you can. Then imagine that pain multiplied on your head and forehead.

I don't mean to preach, but you must understand

what Jesus did for you! Every time you sin, you crucify Him again. And let me say for the record what I know that you already recognize. Premarital sex is sin. But I'd rather you look at it from another perspective. Your Father is King. Not *a* king, but *the* King. That makes you a princess, and that means you are royalty! You deserve only the very best. You deserve the marriage commitment that God intended to come with sex. And you deserve the security that the one you lie down with will still be there in the morning. Then you won't have to worry about whether or not he calls or whether or not someone knows, because he will be your husband. You'll be waking up next to him in the morning and he'll be coming home after work that evening. You deserve that, and if you are with a young man that doesn't understand that you are a princess, then you must demand the respect due a child of the King and you must seriously consider whether or not you want to spend time with a person who underestimates your worth and value!

You really are a special person. God has something special planned for you. Don't let a momentary pleasure ruin your chances of God giving you the very best! Here is another one for you: "We must learn to say no to the good [or perceived good in this case] so that we can say yes to the best."

Princess (hope that nickname has special meaning now), I love you.

Loretta

Are you struggling with homosexuality?
Have you or a close family member been a victim of incest?
Do you feel lonely and abandoned by God?
*Have you recommitted your life to God again and again, yet you
        keep falling?*
If you answered yes to just one of these questions, this chapter is for you.

20s
From a Caribbean Island

I grew up in a conservative Christian home. My mother was a strong, strict, and domineering woman. My father was conservative too. Even though he never went to church with us, he never smoked, drank, or cursed. He had his weaknesses in other ways. My father was incestuous, so he was a little different.

One day, when I was 6 or 7 years old, my sister told me to hide under the bed, watch what happened, and then tell my mother. I slipped under the bed. My father came into the room and said to my sister, "I know you have money." She said that she didn't have any, but he persisted. He was blind at the time, and he touched her as if to suggest that because he couldn't see, he was trying to feel to see where she had hidden the money.

It was a horrible experience, watching him touch my

35

sister in all the wrong places. I did tell my mother, and she was very angry with him.

There was no talk of sex in our house, but our household was still intensely sexual, and that environment came to shape what I believed about sex. My father's hypersexual behavior and my mother's unwillingness to address it had a powerful effect on me. I have 18 brothers and sisters, 10 of them from outside the marriage, so all I heard with regard to relationships between men and women was bickering and fighting about his children. Recognizing that he was having sex with my sisters just made it worse. (One of my sisters had a couple abortions as a result of it.)

Everything about sex seemed to be negative. If it had to do with the relationship between a man and a woman, it seemed tainted. I couldn't separate the good from the bad. I couldn't grasp the fact that it was a good thing for a man and woman to be together, but that couple should be husband and wife—not man and mistress, and certainly not father and daughter.

I went to a private religious school. I don't recall having a girlfriend while I was in high school. I did have sex, though. I had a neighbor named Robbie. I couldn't understand what was wrong with me, but knew I had this "thing." I was so confused. And there in the confusion was Robbie. He was my friend. No one knew of our relationship. And I really didn't understand what was going on myself. But our relationship was significant in that it was my first homosexual encounter.

I'm not a very active person, so I never played outdoor games. I prefer a desk. Of course, the other kids called me names and picked on me a lot. Almost every day there was something new, and every day I couldn't wait to get home so I could see my friend Robbie.

From the time I was about 15 or 16 years old, I totally blocked God out of my life. My brother read an article to me that said if a man is born a homosexual he cannot enter the kingdom of heaven. (He may have suspected that something was happening between Robbie and me.) The article stayed in my mind, and as I grew older, I became convinced that I could not have a relationship with God. I felt a great sense of loneliness and abandonment. I didn't feel like I was rejecting God, but that He was discarding me. My nature just prohibited us from having a relationship.

§ § §

During college a pastor tried to reach out to me. We would chat from time to time, and he began getting a little too close to my issues. Part of me really wanted him to just leave me alone. I remember saying to him, "Don't you understand? If I am born this way, then there is nothing that I can do about it." When I turned to walk to my room, he called me back and we started just to chat. From then on, he became my very good friend. And he was the first person that I ever spoke to about "it." Pastor K was a tower of strength during some turbulent years. In a way, college was worse than high school in that I had learned how to play the game (more on the game and its dangers a little later).

That same pastor gave me a book called *Homosexuality: The Open Door*. The book helped me to begin to understand that God loves everyone. It took a long time for me to reshape my thinking, but in time I grew into the concept of God's love and acceptance. I had always gone to church, even when I felt abandoned by God. Eventually I began to love attending church. And as I sat and listened to the sermons, the words got through to me.

It was still very difficult to change the thought processes and tendencies I had developed from childhood. The most difficult part about it is that the wrong thinking has become a part of your overall thought patterns, and it is just not easy to change something that you have believed for so long. Every day you must get up and remind yourself that it is not true. Each day you must try to unlearn all the garbage that has crept into your mind. You can't block the memories from your mind—you must deal with them. For years I had refused to face them.

I did some things that I should not have done to avoid dealing with myself. I always had to have a high. I knew that if I was not high I would have to face myself, and I couldn't do it. I always had to be high—or have a girl. I couldn't be without a girlfriend. (I had to keep up an image. No one had a clue that I was involved in homosexual behavior.) And I always had to be going to clubs or something. It reached a point that I was doing all kinds of horrible things. A group of us guys hung out together all the time. I became very popular on campus and basically hung out with two particular guys and stayed in constant trouble. But even when I partied Saturday night into Sunday morning, I would come home, shower, lie down, and suddenly it was all still there. I couldn't get away from myself.

The worse experience of my college years was a weekend that a friend came to visit and wanted to get together with some girls on Saturday night. I had to do something at church (remember, I never stopped going). So we went there first, then we picked up a girl. It was a terrible evening of sex and a lot of weed. We did this group thing. It bothered me then, and it still upsets me.

The strangest thing happened the next morning. I felt as if a great darkness had dropped over me. It was really bad. I prayed. It was the first time that I really ever prayed, because I just didn't like how I felt. At the time I was not even sensitive to this whole issue of spiritual warfare. But that morning I sensed something supernatural had entered the room. I felt brutally dark and couldn't understand it. My mind raced as I struggled to understand how I could have sunk that low.

I really don't want to get into details, but just keep in mind that as much as there were encounters with women during my college years, I was also involved with men. It was an extremely difficult, stressful, and painful time in my life. But I felt that it was time to make a change.

§ § §

I remember the first time I got baptized. When they called my name and I stood, a current ran across the auditorium. Everybody was saying "amen" and clapping. It just melted my heart. I didn't think that they would respond that way, because by then I had developed the reputation of being a total devil. I got baptized thinking and believing, *OK, that's it, no more problem.* Of course, that wasn't the case, but that baptism still kept me holding on, perhaps by a little string, all these years.

When I came up out of that pool that morning my mind took hold of something that was outside of this world. I never believed that it would happen, but I really felt as if I literally could have heard rejoicing in heaven. It was a very sincere moment for me. But in a few weeks I was back in the clubs.

Baptism dealt with just one aspect of my life. Not to downplay its importance, but at that time the only thing that it did was to help me see that perhaps I could have a relationship with God. Still that was extremely important, given my prior belief that God didn't want anything at all to do with me. But it didn't do anything else. It never addressed the issues, and I had so many. Pastor K was still hanging in there with me. In all honesty, there was a slight downside to my relationship with him, because sometimes I think he was a little too lenient. He never told me the straight facts with any power or conviction. It was always "God does not abandon. God loves you." He should have been a bit more blunt, should have said, "Harrison, you have to fight this thing." And he should have made the realities of heaven and Jesus more real. Never did he say, "Harrison, if you don't straighten up, you will be lost." Instead, he focused only on the loving nature of God.

Just a few short weeks after I was baptized I went back to the same old lifestyle. Actually, I got worse. I started to smoke and drink even more. Trying to maintain the image of being a macho guy, I began to date lots of women. And there was always lots of weed. One time there were four of us playing truth or dare. I dared the girl my friend liked to kiss him, and she did. Then I dared her to go a little further and a little further. They ultimately had sex. I did a lot of this stuff because I was looking for total acceptance from my friends, who still had absolutely no idea that I was a homosexual.

Then there was BJ—he is dead now.

How we met is kind of strange. For a while, every time I looked up BJ was there. It was as if he was following me around. One day I was walking somewhere and he offered me a ride. I accepted and we became "friends." He was one of the guys I had a sexual encounter with. Understand that I never had real relationships with men. I never had them calling me or coming to my house. Never did I let myself get into a situation where a guy could say, "This is my 'boyfriend'," or what have you. I just couldn't do that. Irrespective of everything that was happening, I couldn't accept the fact that a man would be referring to me as—well, let me just say that I couldn't deal with that "boyfriend" thing. That was too much for me.

Also you have to realize that I was living in the Caribbean. It is a very conservative place, and you have to be extremely careful. Society there is not as tolerant as here in the United States. People from that particular island will kill you over the issue. That's just how it is. They will find you, they will severely injure you, and they will kill you. So the homosexual lifestyle is not a continuous thing. It is like a drug that you take every two or three months.

I remember that I was really depressed (and in need of a fix so to speak) when I picked up the phone and called BJ. Whoever answered said that he was dead. That really blew my mind. The only thing I knew of that could kill someone so quickly was HIV. No one ever told me point-blank that he had it, but then his mother (I think that's who answered the phone) was not apt to tell me. I must tell you, it really devastated me. And even after years of feeling lonely and abandoned, this pain was deeper than anything I had ever experienced, because I felt that I could not share it with anyone.

I think I prayed literally for two weeks straight. During the whole two-week period I doubt that I slept 12 hours. Right through the night I prayed. It began to show on my face that I was greatly distressed, but I had to get up the courage to have an HIV test done. It was as if I had been told I was dying. I went through the whole process. Denial, acceptance, bargaining, and all of that stuff.

Eventually I couldn't handle it alone and went to the person on campus that I thought maybe I could talk to. She seemed to be a very Christlike woman. I told her what the situation was, and she decided to fast and pray for me. Then I got the courage to go to the doctor and have the AIDS test done. While I was there, they told me that a young man had just been diagnosed and had recently died. It was BJ. That was very painful, just knowing for sure. Then I had to wait for the results of my own test. Finally they told me that the test was negative. I didn't have HIV. I went home and called the woman who had been praying. She said that she knew that the test would be negative. I was extremely grateful!

I prayed so much during that time that I didn't even understand what was happening myself. Someone said that they noticed a glow about me. I guess it was because I had been connected to God. I got baptized (once more) and I vowed that "it" would never happen again. I was through with the sex, drugs, everything. But it *did* happen again.

§ § §

Sex is a powerful thing, and if you're not rooted and grounded in what you believe, you will give in. And that is exactly what happened. I left college, came to America, and things just got out of control. It is easier to lead the homosexual lifestyle here in America. By and large, Americans are more tolerant. I used to go to lots of parties. My mind was very vulnerable, and I worked in a field that put me in questionable places. I slid back into the club scene. The frequency of my sexual encounters increased, and I became more disgusted with myself. It is a highly addictive lifestyle. One of the things that I want you to understand is that it separates you both from people and from God. It isolates your mind from His. I needed help.

Trying to find someone to give me support, I called a pastor who had come to my school to do a revival, but it was a dead end. Then I phoned another pastor. (Just let me say that I have no respect for pastors who shy away from tough issues.) I left messages, but my calls weren't returned. Pastors would promise to get information for me and never follow up. Many were concerned that I might take a gun to my head and blow my brains out or be suicidal in some other way. But when they realized that I was more stable than that they would back away. Finally I met a minister that was at least willing to talk. When he asked me what I was doing to help myself, I told him that I had some of Colin Cook's cassettes. The first thing he told me was that Cook had fallen back into homosexuality. Naturally, I was disappointed. The tapes had been helping me, and I couldn't believe that it would be the first thing the pastor would say to me. He never even provided me any alternative support.

Nothing was happening. For a period of several months I tried everything and talked to everybody. I asked Roger Morneau (the author of *Incredible Answers to Prayer* and other books) to put me on his prayer list, and he responded. But the more I tried to find pastoral help, the more frustrated I became.

Finally I met Sister Nemrac. I said to myself that here was somebody who believes that the gospel can work. She believes that it is alive and working, even today! When I look around many churches, I don't see a whole lot that indicates that people feel that the gospel still has power. That made me really observe her for a while. In the meantime, things got worse. I will spare you the details, but it was very ugly. I was out of control.

One night I came home and just started to cry. Also I had begun to reach out even more. I felt that if I would make the first effort, God would help. I got in touch with Sister Nemrac. She invited me to a prayer conference, and that is where my life began to change. However, it was a very difficult period from the time I went to the prayer conference to my (for real this time, final) baptism.

You have to understand that when this thing grabs you, it holds you and seems to bind you in such a way that your conscious mind shuts down and something else takes over. I have often wondered if something just kind of gives in without my even knowing it's happening. While I believe that sin is sin, I also feel that there are certain things that cause you more pain than others. This homosexuality thing—it permeates your soul. It is very important that you recognize that it does not only affect how you think on the surface and your relationships with people, it changes the way you reason, your perceptions. It creeps into your soul.

I went to a prayer conference and felt moved, but not to any great degree. I didn't make any major life changes. However, as I began to attend additional prayer conferences, God just started little by little to soften my heart and speak to me until finally I got baptized. At one prayer conference Randy Maxwell was the presenter. It was very good, because for a moment while I was there I really let go. I let go and I let God. I could feel these little tinglings and knew the Holy Spirit was working. It was good. That all happened very recently. That is why I now have to tread very softly.

After that prayer conference I learned to claim deliverance, to live in the reality of deliverance. But that does not say that temptation won't attack me again. As I kept studying, I recognized that Paul talks about the fact that temptation will come, but that God's grace will keep you from falling (2 Cor. 12:9, 10).

It is all about making new memories. Of course, the sensual and the carnal will always try to force their way into your mind, but if you make new positive memories, you will have something to draw upon. Also I fast sometimes three, four, or five days straight. Once I attempted to go seven days, but Aunt CJ provided a fantastic meal, so I broke my fast after 5 days.

To grasp where I am now, you really have to understand the entire journey. I have mentioned the tapes that I often listen to. They are helpful, because I can relate to them. Everything the speaker said was absolutely true from my perspective. And he went through some Bible verses. I think of Romans 3:23-25 that reminds us that all have sinned and come short of the glory of God, and then the one about propitiation. He reviewed some fundamental issues and talked about some of the feelings you go through, such as that of condemnation, wrath, and abandonment, which is exactly how I was feeling.

I keep going back to this because it is important. Before, I'd felt that God had abandoned me. Now, if I had never been exposed to any biblical teaching, a state of godlessness would not have bothered me, because I would not have had any idea of what the Lord requires through the Bible. But I had been raised a Christian, and the thought of God turning His back on me hurt deeply. The tapes helped me, so I listened to them and studied the Bible, but I didn't have support. In this battle support is vital. So I became disheartened again, and lost my way for a few weeks. But still I continued to pray, to listen to the tapes, and to study.

I'm also looking at the Bible in a different way. In addition, I'm trying to commit verses to memory and trying to pray through them. I think it is Romans 6:13 that says to submit your members as instruments of righteousness unto God. Members means what you are made up of. Look at your members. Your eyes—what they look at. Your ears and what they hear. Your mouth—what it speaks. And especially your feet and where they walk. So much of this thing is about what you see. You respond more intensely to what you see. As a result, sight will trigger most of the mechanisms that bring about your fall.

At times you really need to talk, and if you don't have that, you will slide right back to where you were. If you don't have the right person to talk to, then you will end up calling the wrong person. I thank God that I do have support now.

Just recently I was going through the book *Homosexuality: The Open Door.* It posed the question "How do you feel before a fall?" That is, do you feel depressed, lonely, anxious? It has been almost always true that I experienced all of those feelings before I succumbed. But support and love can get you through those tough times.

§ § §

What would I tell others who are struggling with homosexuality? I don't think that there is anything easy to say. Tell them to go to their parents? If their parents are not the kind of people they can talk to, what do they do then? What happens if they tell their parents and receive a negative or even hostile response? There is always the fear that if you tell somebody, he or she will totally reject you. Then you might end up feeling worse than before. Or how can anyone just tell another person to go and pray?

I can't be a hypocrite, can't tell the person to go talk to a parent or a minister or an elder, knowing (at least in my experience) that the response is always going to be negative. And even if the response doesn't appear to be negative, their attitude will tell you otherwise. Such people might not call back, or they might tell you, "OK, I will visit you," then never show up. I think it is that they don't want to be identified with those who have this particular weakness. And besides that, I don't believe that they really think that God can deliver people from it. Now that I have gone through all of that, here is what I would say to a struggling person:

First, it is important for people to know that there is nothing wrong with sex when used appropriately. People just need to be reeducated. But the most important thing to remember is that this is a spiritual battle and that the first weapon is prayer!

I say pray! It requires a lot of determination. You pray and you read the Bible. The memorization of Scripture helps tremendously. One day I was feeling very down and couldn't get rid of the temptation. Everywhere I looked I encountered something that made me want to do it. Of course, I didn't really want to face up to the fact. Now, I don't even pray anymore to not have the temptation. I do something different. I look at a Scripture, such as 2 Corinthians 12:9, which declares:

"My grace is all you need. My power is seen best through people who have limitations. Your handicap will make you depend on me, and that's when you'll be the strongest" (Clear Word). It goes on to say in verse 10: "As strange as it sounds, I'm thankful for the insults, hardships, sufferings, persecutions and all the pain and difficulties I've had for Christ's sake. . . . I praise the Lord for all these trials. When I realize my own weakness, then I'm the strongest in Christ" (Clear Word). I think it is 1 Corinthians 10:13 that says: "Also remember that you haven't had any temptation that other people haven't had. God is faithful and He will not let you be tempted beyond your strength but will provide a way of escape so you'll be able to overcome" (Clear Word).

One particular evening I couldn't shake the temptations. Even listening to the tapes didn't help. I just couldn't get rid of what was happening in my mind. So I prayed and went to bed. The next morning I did my studies again and felt a little better. However, as soon as I walked out the door, Satan attacked my mind. Then I rememberd my Bible verses. I think it was Revelation 3:10 that came to mind: "Since you have kept my commandments . . . I will be with you as you go through the time of trouble" (Clear Word). As I recalled the texts I felt peace in my heart and was able to get through the crisis.

This is something that must be fought totally and completely from a spiritual perspective. We cannot deal with it any other way. The memorization of Scripture is particularly important. Ask the Father to help them become alive in your mind. You must guard and fortify your mind with them.

And speaking of guarding your mind, television is so

saturated with sex that you need to get rid of it. The same thing applies to most popular magazines. You have to eliminate anything that might be detrimental to your spiritual health—even heterosexual materials. Whatever they might be, if there is a possibility that the contents could be tempting or distracting in any way, then they must go! Next, don't fantasize through masturbation. I would say throw away any secular music that stimulates the sexual imagination. Never let your guard down on anything. You have to be so careful. I don't even go to the beach—haven't been to one in years. God's work in the life is a cleansing process, and this time I am allowing God to clean me up for real!

God and My Parents Were Right After All

Reesa's Story

"We love each other and are committed to each other, so it is OK to have sex."
"I'll wait till I am 50 to have sex in the framework of marriage."
"The older I get the smarter my parents get."
"I want my own apartment; I can take care of myself and make my own decisions."
"I'm a virgin again, and it's harder the second time around."
Read Reesa's story to understand these seemingly conflicting statements.

Very conservative family
Consistently attended church
East and West Indian heritage

D ear God, it's me again. But I am serious this time, and I come in the name of Jesus. I have so much to pray about. So many hurts, so many issues, so many regrets. So, God, if You will be patient with me, we can talk about all of these things. Then I can get them off my chest and allow Your power to fill my life. Lord, I want to go through each aspect of my life with You to give it to You. To ask for Your forgiveness and then move on.

So, Lord, I begin by asking forgiveness for the way that I rebelled against my parents. You know it was hard, because they were so different. It was as if they were in a time warp of sorts. I know that culture had a lot to do with it. My parents wanted to bring our double Indian heritage here to America. Brought up under the strictest of circumstances in an arranged marriage, they were so family oriented that they never even let us spend the night at anyone's house or allowed us to have friends over. And boyfriends (yeah, right!) was out of the question.

One day my younger sisters and I just packed our bags and left. What pain that must have been for them as parents. I thank You for my mom who found out where we were and came to check on us. Even in her hurt and disappointment she showed love. Thank You, God. Her heart must have broken every time she drove up to the trailer. Yeah, it was a double-wide trailer with three bedrooms and two baths, but still it was no place for us to be living. We should have been at home. I thank You, Lord, that my sisters got smart and went back home. Who knows what could have happened to them. I caused so much stress and strain on my parents. I was stupid, and I don't understand what happened to me between the ages of 16 and 19. I was going through so much, trying to figure out who I was. I thought that I was grown and that I knew it all. Of course, now I sit embarrassed and in need of Your forgiveness for my foolishness.

But, Lord, that's not it (as if You don't already know). Then there is the whole boyfriend thing. I never meant to get sexually involved with Nick. I was 18, still stupid and thinking that I knew it all. Thank You for protecting me even in my foolishness. Forgive me, God, but You know that when I became sexually active with him a year or so after we started to date, I really thought that he was the guy I was going to marry. You also know that I didn't consciously plan to have sex with him. It was very spontaneous on both our parts. We were at his mom's house and one thing just led to another.

I lacked understanding in so many ways, because my parents never really talked to me about the subject, but I knew enough that he had to wear a condom. Lord, I realize that You already know all this stuff, but I just need to say it. Thanks for listening. Anyway, God, You recognize that the thing I hated most was those visits to the clinic. It was some public health place. They asked lots of questions, gave out condoms, and, of course, the whole PAP smear thing was just pure torture. And after all that they look at you and ask the "code" question: "Are you interested in family planning?" That really meant Do you want birth control pills? I said yes.

There I was walking out of the clinic with pills in one hand and a bag of condoms in the other, yet You never turned Your back on me. It was terrible, and I really messed myself up playing around with those pills, trying to play catch up after forgetting to take them sometimes for two weeks straight. I would take three pills a day. My menstrual cycle, my body—everything was just out of whack because of that. Forgive me, Lord, for needing the pills in the first place. The tears flow freely as I think about my inconsistency, the resulting pregnancy scares, and how disappointed You must have been.

Worrying about getting pregnant is so draining, so stressful. Then, because I was so stressed and worried, my period ended up being irregular and that just caused more stress. I hated the whole scene. I couldn't deal with the headaches and pressure, because I was think-ing, *Am I pregnant? What am I going to do?* I worried what people would say. *If I am—do I go through the abortion thing? Where do I get the money from? Do I tell him?* But as stressful, frightening, and embarrassing as the false alarms were, the really bad thing was that as soon as I found out I wasn't pregnant, I went right back to having sex again. Lord, "I am sorry" seems so inadequate. But I am. Forgive me.

Lord, I have to be honest and say that I often wonder why You didn't intervene. If my first sexual experience had been a bad one (as many say it can be), maybe I would have thought about it more. For me, being sexual meant that there was an emotional attachment. It wasn't something that I did just because it felt right. Sex with him was comfortable. I wasn't out there with a bunch of different guys, but with my boyfriend, the person that I loved and who loved me. Our relationship was stable, so sex didn't devastate me or anything. But Lord, little did I realize that it was the beginning of some horrible times. I just can't help but wonder how things would have been different if my first sexual experience had been a bad one.

I am not questioning You, Lord. Just talking to You about me. Interestingly enough, though, the first negative thing that happened as a result of having sex is that I just got sick and tired of the fact that every time we got together that is all Nick wanted to do. I would ask, "Why do you always want to have sex?"

He would say, "Because I don't ever see you, and this is the way I express myself."

I would reply, "Well, why can't you express yourself some other way?"

Although I got really tired of it, it was not easy to escape the relationship. The situation got very ugly. Thank You for protecting me. And thank You for loving me in spite of me.

Then, Lord, as if I was a child swinging to the opposite extreme, I decided to go the other direction and just chill out with guys without getting into serious relationships. That's where Lee came in. All I can say is Please keep Your promise to throw my sins into the deepest parts of the sea. I thought it was cool for a while. No commitment, no stress. We just had sex when we felt like it. I didn't see him often. When I wanted to, I looked him up, and when he wanted to see me, he called. I thought I didn't care about the relationship until after so many times of being together I started to feel emotionally attached. Lord, I wish I could tell other young women that a lot of times they don't realize that when you give yourself sexually, you are giving more than you realize.

You make yourself open, totally vulnerable emotionally and mentally as well as physically too. But that fact didn't sink in until years later. Girls don't recognize how much of themselves they are giving when they choose to sleep with somebody. I got hurt because I became emotionally attached to him even though I tried to be tough and nonchalant about it. So I tried to let it go, let it ride. After a while I broke off the relationship, because I wanted more than just sex. I—I was hurt, really disappointed, because we no longer even saw each other. It left me with a sense of being used and feeling really small. That breakup was another emotional roller coaster that dropped my self-esteem to an all-time low. I didn't understand who I was and certainly didn't understand that I was Your child and of great value to You.

And the thing is, Lord, I found that I didn't take the time out to realize or to recognize what I wanted out of life. In a sense I was running from myself (instead of running to You, Lord). I was always on the go, trying to hang out, party, drink, and everything else. It was just one thing after the other until finally I came to my senses and realized that there is something more to life. It became clear at that point that I should have been seeking a committed relationship with You, not the guy that I had been having sex with. Now I know that sex is good in only one relationship—marriage.

Lord, I can hear the church members talking now. "What was she thinking about? Didn't she know about the consequences?" You know that I didn't think that there would be consequences. He and I didn't plan it and probably, if I had given it just a little thought, I would have said no. Especially if I had considered the future and that my husband would have to deal with the fact that his wife had already been with all these different men. Maybe then it wouldn't have happened. But at that age you don't sit down and think about the future. I chose to have sex with Daniel because I honestly thought we were so deeply in love that I knew he would be the person that I was going to be with the rest of my life. And we had a beautiful relationship. I didn't have any regrets about that, but I would have waited to have sex.

If I realized then what I know now, I would have said to him, "If you love me that much, then wait for me, nurture me, help me." But I wasn't thinking at all. I just wanted to show him how much I loved him. Caught up in the relationship, I ignored possible consequences until I became afraid that I was pregnant, and I certainly never considered the danger of sexually transmitted diseases! Oh, God, what was I doing? I desecrated my body, Your temple.

Lord, I still remember it as if it were yesterday, that

first time that I encountered an STD. As I sat in that hated clinic, the nurse said to me, "You have gonorrhea."

"What?" I asked, not even knowing such a thing existed. She gave me a big pamphlet. As I read, my eyes fell on the words "sexually transmitted disease" and I was shocked and furious! The sad thing is that I went through that scenario a few times with the same guy. When I would tell him to get checked, he would claim that he had, then a few months later I would end up with the same thing again. Up to this point I had never been exposed to STDs and really had no clue what they were. Now, all of a sudden I found myself thrown into this situation, looking for someone to blame, but I couldn't get mad at anybody but myself. I had to face reality. If this guy could give me gonorrhea, he could infect me with AIDS. So just before I left for college, I took an AIDS test to make sure I was OK. Six months later I had another one just to follow up. Fortunately I was HIV negative.

Thank You, Lord, and please forgive me again. How stupid could I be? Not thinking rationally, I persuaded myself that I was in love with this person. Now that I consider it, I realize that I could be sick from HIV or even dead. I took chances with my life—and it wasn't even mine to play around with. I am so sorry, Lord.

And thank You for helping me to reflect on my life while I was in college. You sent me there to get my life together spiritually. It isn't that I didn't go to church before then. But I attended just to please the adults in my life. I would stay out late, go to church, and as soon as the service was over, I was out of there. For that I am sorry as well. Each week You tried to speak to me, but each week I ignored Your voice. Forgive me, Lord.

It feels so good to let You lead in my life, and it is so

wonderful to know that Your Holy Spirit is working in me, with me, and through me. Thank You!

God, I remember many nights when all I felt like doing was just crying. I would think back on all my sins and guilt and plead, "Lord, please take it away." I had so much guilt and so much hurt. Finally You helped me to realize that You love me and that all I need to do is confess and You will truly wash my sins away. Please, cast them into the deepest parts of the sea. Thank You, God, for that assurance. You know I wouldn't trade anything for that. I wouldn't want to lose the peace of mind that I have now to go back and experience any of that again.

There's nothing in the world that I want except You. That is not to say I don't slip up. But God, my plan is to live my life for and with You. Yes, I may still mess up and fall flat on my face. That is when I find myself weeping as I beg and plead for forgiveness. Sex is a deep and powerful thing, Lord, and I want to help other young women understand that sex is for marriage—period.

I have to talk about Sammy. My first Christian boyfriend, he wanted to be a pastor. It started out as a wonderful relationship and was so different. Ours was a spiritual high. We prayed together and read the Bible together. Such things in a relationship were new to me, and I enjoyed them to the fullest. I had high expectations—after all, I was dating a Christian man—and assumed that we were going to have a pure, heavenly relationship. Boy, was I wrong!

Lord, even though it is painful, I have to confess it and go on. The first time we had sex we were in a hotel. You know we didn't get a room with intentions of having sex, but someone had come to visit Sammy and had a hotel room. One night I was there (which was the first mistake). We were sleeping in the same bed (the second mistake), and one thing led to another until we had sex. Of course we felt extremely guilty afterward. As Your Holy Spirit worked on me, we prayed and confessed our sin before You. We knew that it was not right in Your sight and were really sorry. But not sorry enough to stop. We did it again and again. It wasn't as often as in some of the other relationships, but it was still wrong and we realized that. We didn't make it a habit, because both of us knew that it wasn't what we wanted to do. What can I say, Lord? You sent me to a Christian college to get my life in order, but I fell right back into the same foolishness.

Lord, I so desperately want to tell other young women about the consequences of sex outside of marriage. If You give me an opportunity, I will tell them, "Don't put yourself in a compromising situation." I would say, "You have to be honest with yourself. If you know that you don't want to have sex or you realize that you are weak in that area, you just have to be cautious and don't let yourself get in a situation in which one thing leads to another."

I would tell them, "Don't give in on the spur of the moment." Wait until you get married. Sex, once you experience it, becomes a natural drug to the body. It is like a craving. Once you have had it, you keep wanting it and wanting it and wanting it. Before you know it, your urge for sex is out of control. The bottom line is *wait.*

God, it feels as if I have come full circle. People told me to wait and I didn't listen, yet now here I am saying the same thing. But the difference is that I didn't have anyone that I could talk to, because sex was such a taboo thing. People—especially parents—seem to think that if they don't talk about sex, then it will just go away. I, on the other hand, am saying not to do it, but I am also sharing the mistakes of my personal experience. Thank You for making me willing to be honest and tell people what You have done in my life.

And because You have made such an awesome difference in my life, Lord, I am a virgin for the second time around. You know I wouldn't make the same decision again. I would wait for sex till I am 50 (or older). Yes, I am pure in Your sight. My sins are on the bottom of the sea.

And the challenges are much different. The curiosity factor is gone, the rebellion has disappeared, and the "I'll do it to prove my love" is certainly not an issue these days. I am smarter than that. And even though all that is true and I have the benefit of my mistakes, it is still hard, Lord, and I am asking that You will continue to give me the strength to stand for You. Some of the things You have directed me to do require discipline. You have instructed me to keep my physical body in shape, directed me to exercise. Also You have told me to go about being celibate with the same passion that I had sex. I must take a firm stand for what I know is right and not let anybody or anything make me turn away from You.

I give You thanks because You have assured me that You love me and that if I fall (not that I am supposed to do it on purpose), You will be right there to pick me up, dry my tears, and forgive me again. God, my intention is to make You proud of me. I know now that You are my friend and that only You can love me unconditionally. This time, I am changing my lifestyle for both of us. I don't want to do anything to hurt You, because I know that I am Your child. Lord, You have taught me to love and respect myself.

But You will have to direct me on this. Even as I

pray, Your Holy Spirit whispers the right answer in my ear. My friends tell me that I should always carry a condom just in case. Lord, for the record I want to say here and now that I will never do that. To me, that is just a ploy of Satan to plant in my mind the idea that I "might" need to use one. What I need is Your help. You have been with me so far, so please don't leave me now.

Finally, Lord, I want to say what I realize You knew all along. God, You and my parents were right after all!

One Dark and Stormy Night

6

Tracie's Story

"If I have sex with him, then he won't break up with me."
"My parents don't care anyway."
"I really don't like sex, but I keep doing it."
This chapter is for you if you have made, or even thought, just one of the above statements.

Late 20s
Raised in what was supposed to be a Christian home
Parents divorced
Decided at a young age to have sex

My parents divorced when I was pretty young, and for the next four or five years we children were basically on our own. In our house it was Do what you want and fend for yourself. My dad was gone, and my mom was working (and having her share of fun too).

No one sat me down and talked to me about sex. I don't remember exactly how I learned, but more than likely it was from what I call "kissin' cousins." You know, those children that you experiment with? It might be playing house or doctor or just plain kissing. That was my introduction to sex. It started when I was about 7 years old, and although we were always fully clothed, it just served to heighten my sexual curiosity and desire to do and experience more.

I had my first real sexual experience at age 14. I was

"dating" a 17-year-old guy. First of all, I was not allowed to date. Second, my mother told me to stay away from him, and third, he was a real worthless kind of guy who had lots of girlfriends. So why did I have sex with him? Quite simply because I felt that the only way I could get close to him was to give him that part of me which no young woman should give to anyone else except her husband. So we had sex. It was really quite childish. (It was a dark and stormy night . . . Not really, but it makes for a good story line.)

Actually, we would sneak home from high school. The first time we were at my house, and it was a painful experience—probably why I didn't like it. It certainly was not compassionate, and for sure it wasn't lovemaking. I was just trying to hold on to a 17-year-old guy. Although I really didn't like sex, I continued having it with him for about a year and a half. Ultimately, I went to the clinic for some birth control pills. (Of course, I had to sneak there or my mother would have killed me.) I was sure that if I got pregnant my mother would have thrown me out.

After a year and a half the relationship ended. I was very sad, not because of missing the sex, since I didn't like it anyway, but I knew I would miss what I thought was love. By that time I had been fatherless for several years and was searching for love and comfort. In addition, some other things going on at home were really stressful. I needed some consistency and love from my parents—especially my father. What I got was sex with a 17-year-old.

Although I was in no hurry to get involved again, I did start dating a guy during my junior year in high school. He was a Christian and I was a Christian and we were trying to do what was right. Although we dated for three years, we never had sex, and I felt good about it.

Even after I went to college I didn't have sex for two more years. That made a total of five years. I was doing well and was quite proud of myself. Then I met a guy named Obie, who became a part of my life for four years. The reason that we broke up after four years? Sex. I didn't really like sex and knew that it wasn't a part of God's plan outside marriage. The first time we had sex I cried, and each time after that I would get mad at him. We would break up for a week or two and pray and repent and promise that we would never do it again . . . and then "it" would happen again. I would become angry at him, and we wouldn't speak to each other for a while. Every time we had a major argument or problem it was because he knew that I didn't want to have sex and he did.

He was really trying to stop, but I believe it is harder for men. This cycle of us having sex, me getting mad, and the two of us praying went on for four years. Finally, I decided that we should see other people. Truth be told, sex was controlling our relationship, and I needed to get out. I honestly believe that had we not had sex we would have married and had a lasting relationship.

If I describe the years with Obie as stressful, I'd have to call the breakup downright traumatic. I wanted to be with him, but the sex thing was killing me. Even though I was the one to initiate the breakup, I still didn't want him to be with anyone else (especially since I knew he would be having sex). It was a horrible period in my life. The relationship without sex would have been so different and so much better.

After that I just kind of took it easy for a while. Eventually, I ended up spending time with a good friend from college. More like siblings than anything else, we started to hang out together and just had lots of fun. It was nice and very comfortable—until the sex thing raised its head again. Now, keep in mind that we were good friends and used to lie on the bed and laugh and talk and watch TV or whatever and nothing ever happened. After we dated probably for about six months, one dark and stormy night (for real this time) we had sex.

Three months later I decided I was going to start taking the pill, but he was insecure and felt really bad about the fact that we were having sex anyway (we were both Christians and regularly attending church at the time). He asked me not to take the pill, and I agreed. The very next month I got pregnant. We were in love and were already planning to get married, so we decided to hurry things up.

Lest people think that my experience is a "happily ever after" and try to use the old "she did it and turned out OK" excuse, let me break this thing down. I gave away at 14 years of age the only thing that even God could not fully return—my virginity. If you lose money, He can replace it and give you even more. The same with property. Self-respect, honor, dignity, all can be restored. Virginity cannot. Yes, you can become pure before the Lord, make a vow of chastity, and move on—confident that God has forgiven—and that is important to do. But the virginity, the innocence, has vanished forever.

The other thing is an even bigger problem. When you have premarital sex, it really mixes up your mind when it comes time for you to have sex with your spouse. Comparison and contrast is a natural part of life. If you have a slice of pie at my house and then go to someone else's home and have another slice, you cannot help but compare. In a similar way you contrast the personalities of the people you date and compare their styles of clothing, etc. It is just natural to judge in terms of sex as well. But that is not a good thing. You start saying to yourself, "Is my spouse as good as this one or that one?" That is why God intended for you to have sex with just one person, your spouse. A lot of times people fall into extramarital relationships, because they do have something to compare to. They start to think about other people that they have been with. Sometimes, people will ask their spouses to do certain things that they have done with other people. It is just not a pretty picture, and I have had plenty of stress in my marriage as a result of my premarital sexcapades.

Would I do it again? Absolutely not! Do I have any regrets? Yes, I do. I wish I had never had any other experiences to compare my husband to. And I wish that on my wedding night I had been nervous about having sex for the first time instead of being pregnant and thinking, *Been there, done that. Let's just get some sleep.*

Trust me on this—sex is for married people. Wait for it. It is worth it. Within marriage, it is wonderful and beautiful. Outside of marriage it raises just too many issues and consequences, including the one that is yelling "mommy" right now, so let me wrap this up by saying that premarital sex is not worth losing your virginity and your innocence on a dark and stormy night or even a bright and sunny day for that matter!

Strange but True

7

Toby's Story

"I am a Christian young man."
"I will not 'do it' just because everyone else is."
"I choose to wait, even though it is difficult sometimes."
"My wife will be my first, by God's grace."
Toby has made a promise to himself to wait until he is married. It is a rare thing today, considering that Toby is in his 20s already. Read his story for solid advice on how to hold out.

Male
Mid-20s
Canadian
Raised in Christian home

My name is Toby, and I'm a 25-year-old Christian man who is waiting until marriage to have sex. It may sound strange, but it is certainly true, and I want to tell you why I am postponing it, and how I've been successful up to this point.

But first a little about my background. My parents have been married for more than 30 years, and I have one brother. I attended public schools and consistently went to church as a child. I would describe my family as conservative, and although my parents are of a minority that have remained married, our family is not perfect by any means. My parents didn't sit down with me and tell me the facts about sex, but they stressed high morals in every facet of life.

I guess I learned about sexuality from being exposed to different things at school. Of course, TV played a part, and our home had plenty of James Dobson books. Because when I was very young lots of kids were being kidnapped, raped, and molested, my parents often approached the topic from the perspective of safety. I recall them saying such things as: "Don't let people bother you or touch you inappropriately, etc." Also there was always a steady theme of waiting until marriage for consensual sex and, of course, the books *What Every Young Man Should Know About Sex* and the corresponding one for women as well. I think that I was pretty well educated about sex. Between the health classes at school, the moral training at home, and the general sense of right and wrong that I developed, I made a conscious decision not to engage in premarital sex.

I don't really recall how old I was, but from the time I understood the concept of premarital sex and why I should wait, I embraced the idea of postponing sex until marriage. I decided to "reserve myself until marriage," to use a quote from the values/goals page of my daily planner. I chose to wait for two reasons. First of all, God said to! Second, because I want my wife to be the first and only person with whom I have sex. And now that I think about it, I guess there is also a third reason: I want to keep the commitment that I made to myself.

Now, let's talk a little about the "how."

I generally date young women who have the same values as I do. Most of the time they belong to my religious affiliation. Always, they are Christians.

Let me just say a word about how we as Christians deal with sex. More often than not we emphasize the "don't have sex" part and in many cases don't give any standards or guidelines as to "how far is too far."

Let me share an experience with you. Well, actually, I don't want to, but I think that it is necessary to illustrate my point. Believe me, I would much rather approach this from a philosophical perspective. I would love to speak from the experiences of others rather than sharing my own. In all honesty, I am not sure that I am ready or willing to reveal the most vulnerable stories. But I will, because I know that it will help others.

I will describe a progression in which I set limits for myself and then broke those limits with each encounter. Ultimately, I came very close to shattering my vow to myself, my future wife, and my God! And in the process, I learned that I am not as strong as I thought. What stopped us? Two things: we both knew it was something that we didn't want to do, and she didn't want to take my virginity. She said that she would hate herself for that. (It's something you don't hear very often—a woman worrying about taking a man's virginity.) The bottom line here is that too far, in many cases, depends upon the people involved. Anything that starts the hormones pumping is cause for concern. That might be a touch, a kiss, or an embrace.

Here is what happened in my case. First of all, I am not a "thrill of the moment, it just happened" person. With me it is "I care about this person so much; how can I hold back a part of myself when I want to make her completely happy?" In many cases that perspective is worse than the "thrill of the moment" perspective, because it sounds more noble and respectable. It makes having sex extremely easy, because it is so well rationalized. When Lisa and I lost control and almost had sex shortly afterward, we did three things. First, we sincerely prayed about it. Second, we talked about it, and third, we decided that we would cooperate with God, understanding that if we chose to put ourselves in situations where sexual activity was likely to take place, then we were saying no to God and yes to self and sin and Satan. We made it plain and simple—if we started taking off our clothes, we were saying no to God.

Once I was with a girl (we basically had no clothes on) when she said, "You're holding me the way a man should hold his wife." That really made me think. Mind you, we weren't really doing anything. It was just that we were doing too much for people who had committed themselves to not having premarital sex. And too much for people who were not married. God sets the principles down, and when we try to see how close to the fire we can get without being burned, we're putting ourselves at risk. Let me tell you, I am still suffering from smoke inhalation from that incident. I have no desire to play with fire again.

Despite the fact that I consider myself to be very controlled, I recognize that I don't have as much self-control as I think. So I need to play safe. That means I don't put myself into situations where I am at risk of messing up. We all have different capacities for restraint. Each person must determine his own limits. However, *it is safer to set the limit on the conservative side than to discover what the limit should have been as you pass it.* It is also important to know for yourself why you set the limit where you did and why you don't want to have sex prior to marriage.

Couples need to set boundaries, communicate them to each other, and agree on them. As the relationship progresses, both parties—not just one—should be responsible for upholding the limits. Also, it is obvious that they should avoid high-risk situations. People generally have a problem with this, because they infer from such a statement that there can be no intimacy at all. However, I tend to disagree. Relationships are about intimacy, and intimacy doesn't have to be a sexual thing. Intimacy involves closeness—spiritual and emotional. It is about trust and caring, about being comfortable with someone, knowing that you can be vulnerable with them and not have to worry about what they might do to you.

It bothers me that people often define intimacy and closeness as having sex. When, in fact, sex is an outgrowth of mental, emotional, spiritual, and physical intimacy. All aspects should be present within the marriage bond before sex occurs.

8

70 Times 7 and Counting

Barbara's Story

Barbara felt so guilty about her sex life that she stopped attending church. She thought she had messed up too much for God to forgive her. So many people looked up to her, and she felt as if she had let them all down. But she found that in God there is hope, even when you make mistakes again and again.

Barbara
Female
First had sex at 18
Raised in a strict Christian home
Second-time-around virgin

Dear Loretta:

We were the church couple—the ones everyone looked up to. After discussing it, we decided sex was not a part of the plan. And for the longest time, we walked the straight and narrow. Then one night when we ended up alone in his apartment, things got pretty hot and heavy. Before we got to the point of no return, we just backed up and kind of pretended that nothing had happened. Both of us knew that we had gone too far, but we never talked about it, which caused problems later on. After all, how do you say to the other person that you're not coming over because of that thing you never discussed? So we just stayed away from each other until the shock of that night wore off.

I'm still not sure when we changed our minds. But one Saturday night one thing led to another. You would think that we would have learned our lesson from that previous episode, but instead we found ourselves going even further than we did the first time—and we had sex. I excused myself with the fact that we really did love each other and had been together for almost two years. Afterward we talked about it and swore that we wouldn't do it again, but we did—again and again and again. Once you've been there it's hard to stop. I never used any form of birth control, because I never really planned to have sex. It just happened. One minute we would be surrounded by people, then the next minute we were alone the inevitable occurred. I thought that using birth control would brand me as "one of those bad girls who had sex all the time." I tried to make myself feel better by never bothering with it at all.

To make matters worse, I had given my all (and I do mean all) to this guy. Playing wife and maid, I cooked dinner, did the laundry—the whole bit. It was a big sacrifice, and I was still in high school. All during this time I was the assistant youth leader at my church, planning programs, working with the younger teens, and feeling as if I was on my way straight to hell. Eventually my boyfriend and I broke up and I went away to college, thinking that I was doomed to be lost because of our sinful relationship. So I just let my relationship with the Lord continue to erode. After all, He was not going to listen to someone who had fallen and prayed and fallen and prayed again and again. Once at college, I didn't go to church, but found myself visiting my friends and the mall when I should have been at worship. It was a dark period in my life.

I wish that I could say that I got myself together after this relationship and walked the straight and narrow, but I didn't. It took pregnancy to force me to put my life together. Well, let me clarify that. I didn't get pregnant, but I thought that I was. I was in a room praying by myself, probably the first time that I ever really prayed. I was just a wreck. My period was late. Although I had prayed many times before and thought I was sincere, now, driven by the fear that I was pregnant, I prayed on another level. Disgusted with myself, having sworn that such a thing would never happen to me, that I would stop having sex, now I was scared to death that I was pregnant. I just knew that this was going to be my punishment.

As I wept my eyes out, I prayed as I had never before. Then something happened. I really felt as if God said to me, "You are going to be all right." I felt truly forgiven. When I got off my knees, I knew that I wasn't pregnant and that He had forgiven me. Until I had sex again.

Loretta, you can't possibly imagine the guilt. I don't really know why I am writing to you. You can't possibly understand. If you have not been there you just have no idea of what it feels like to remember the night before and shudder. To think about your parents, yourself, and God! And how you let all three down. Then there is the feeling that everyone knows what you've done. That somehow people are able to look at you and instantly tell that you're no longer a virgin. And then there is the matter of God.

I said that it just happened—but deep in my heart I knew better. It just felt so good, and I felt so wanted and accepted that I just couldn't stop. Then I was "hooked." We have no real relationship—just have sex as much as we can. I want to stop. I want to get back on track, but I can't. We go out on an innocent date and end up having sex—then we pray and beg God's forgiveness. The cycle has happened more times than I care to remember or admit. At this point I just know that God is through with me, and when I meet the man that I am to marry, I will have to face the fact that I am "used." And that another man has been where only my husband should have been and has done what only my husband should have done.

Guilty as Charged

Dear Forgiven:

No, I'm not responding to the wrong person. I hear you loud and clear and have talked to so many people who have been where you are, but I want you to know, you really *are* forgiven! Jesus Christ died for your sins because He loves you. He wants to forgive you and help you to live in a way that you all (you, Jesus, and your family) will be proud of. Ask Him earnestly and honestly to forgive you. Find a quiet place and spend some time talking to Him. Tell Him what you need and why you feel you long for sex. As a matter of fact, read the letter you wrote to me to Him. Tell Him everything. Spend some time alone and let Him talk to you. Just be quiet in His presence. Look up every text you can about forgiveness. Read every story you can about forgiveness and restoration. The stories of David and Mary Magdalene are excellent starting points. Let God speak to you through the lives of these people.

God constantly reminds us that He will not remember our sins. That He'll cast them into the depths of the sea. If you don't get anything else I say to you, understand this—Jesus wants to forgive you. Just ask Him. Claim Psalm 51 as your own and rejoice in the forgiveness of our Father! I like the way the Clear Word puts it: "Have mercy on me, O God, according to your loving kindness. According to your abundant mercy, blot out my sins. Wash away my guilt and cleanse me from sin. I know my weaknesses, and I am all too conscious of my sinful nature. I have sinned against you and you are the only One who knew about it. What I did in secret was all the more wicked because I knew you were watching me . . . Create in me a clean heart, O God, and put a right spirit within me. Don't ask me to leave your presence and don't take the Holy Spirit away from me. Restore to me the joy of your salvation and grant me a willing heart to obey you. Then I will teach transgressors your ways, and sinners will turn back to you. . . . Only when I am forgiven can I truly open my mouth in praise and tell others about your mercy and your righteousness" (Ps. 51:1-14).

That isn't the entire psalm, but it gives you an idea of the pain of sin that the psalmist experienced. And I love the fact that as he talked to God his words ultimately turned to praise! If you are really serious about this forgiveness thing, take some time to paraphrase the psalm to fit your circumstances. I guarantee you that God will forgive you! And by the way, don't become a scuba diver. God has promised to forgive your sins and cast them into the depths of the sea (Micah 7:19). Let them stay there.

Barbara, when I was in the fourth grade I had a teacher who used to jump up and down in the middle of the classroom, wave her arms frantically, clap her hands, and yell, "Enough is enough." One dreadful day I ended up in her path, and somehow as her flailing arms went down, so did my skirt! (To this day I am not sure how it happened.) But there I stood in the middle of the classroom—white shirt, white slip, super skinny legs, and blue skirt (around my very skinny ankles). It's a day I'd like people to forget.

Sixteen years later I bumped into a classmate, and after the standard greetings, do you have any idea what subject came up? "Hey, Loretta, remember when Mrs. M pulled your skirt down?" Why did he have to remember that very significant source of embarrassment? He could have thought of so many other memorable events, such as the time he got spanked for putting a tack in the teacher's chair, or the time I beat him in the spelling bee, or the time—well, you get the point. If left up to my classmate, that incident would follow me to my grave. I can see the tombstone now.

> We remember Loretta well,
> especially the day her skirt fell.
> She said she'd pay us to forget,
> but she'd pay even more if she could just omit
> "enough is enough," then the wave, then the clap,
> but since that's impossible, think she'd settle for a
> stronger snap?

At this point in my life I am just happy that God, in His omnipotence, does forget. He forgets our sins and all of the embarrassment that we have caused Him. Promising to forgive our iniquity, He vows that He will throw our sins into the depths of the sea and remember them no more. God won't bring up the negatives of the past and remind us of them. Our Saviour has already raised His arms and stretched them out on the cross and proclaimed, "Enough is enough."

Just one more thing. If that boyfriend of yours is not willing to "go and sin no more" as Jesus commanded Mary after He forgave her, then you should drop him like a hot potato. You are on your way to a new life with Christ. Don't let anything or anyone hold you back! Remember, you are forgiven.

Love,
Loretta

Dear Loretta,

It is amazing how one decision can affect you for a long time, especially considering that I never got pregnant or AIDS or anything horrible like that. But let me tell you what is going on with my new boyfriend. He is a wonderful Christian guy and a virgin, if you can believe that. We have a good relationship and have been talking about marriage. I have been true to God and myself and have not had sex since I made my last and final commitment. I told Kevin about my past. Unfortunately, he has a real problem with it. I guess he always wanted to marry a virgin since he has been able to hold out so long. His response was, "I can't believe that you did this to me."

For a long time I felt guilty and unworthy of being with him, but God got me straight on that. I told Kevin that I didn't even know him at the time and that it was my decision and certainly had nothing to do with him. The whole thing was my mistake and my cross to bear. It was a long time ago, and I made my peace with God. He took my sins and buried them in the depths of the sea and then washed me as white as snow. If that isn't good enough for him, I said, then he doesn't need to be with me, because that is about as clean as I'm going to get! It may sound rude, but I was just sick and tired of him bringing up my past. Do you think I did the right thing?

Barbara:

No, I don't *think* you did the right thing—I *know* you did! Remember, I told you not to go deep-sea diving for your own sins, and by all means don't let anyone else do it either. You deserve the very best, and if Kevin can't accept that you are a changed person, especially since it all happened before you knew him, then I will caution you that maybe other issues might arise in your relationship that he will have a hard time getting past as well. Think about it.

The other side of that coin is that you made some decisions that have consequences. We can be thankful that God is forgiving, and you must always remember that you are forgiven. Yet you must never forget that all of our actions have consequences, and Kevin's reaction is one of them. It is wonderful that you didn't get pregnant or contract a sexually transmitted disease, but there are so many more consequences that we just don't think about. Please, as you talk to your friends who are already having sex, or those who may be thinking about becoming sexually active, tell them of some of the "hidden" consequences.

You are moving in the right direction. Keep up the good work and keep as close to God as you can!

All my love and support,
Loretta

Beat Down, but Not Destroyed

Andrea's Story

Have you ever asked the question "How far is too far?"
Do you think that the answer to premarital sex is to go as far as you can and do as much as you can while remaining a "technical" virgin?
Are you considering living with your boyfriend?
Do you think that "nice girls" don't get venereal diseases?
If you answered yes to any of the above questions, you need to read this chapter.

Andrea
Waited for marriage to have sex (technically)
Religious family
Single parent

I was eight months pregnant and waddling (I was so big that they thought I was having twins). I knew that the whole situation was wrong and that I shouldn't have been living with him in the first place. Now, fed up with the whole situation, I couldn't find the suitcases, but I didn't care at that point. I was getting out!

Yari was mad because I was leaving him instead of him throwing me out. Furious as he walked up the basement steps behind me, he shoved his chest against my back, trying to intimidate me. When I turned around to push him away, he grabbed me and tried to swing me down the stairs. As I held on to his coat, he started strangling me. I fell down. Yanking me up, he swung me around and my head went through the Sheetrock on one side. Then he hurled me the other way, and I almost went over the railing. One last push, and my head went through the Sheetrock again.

As I crawled up the steps on my belly, sobbing, I thought to myself, *I am a college graduate and from a respectable Christian family. How did I get here? I didn't get raped by a drug dealer or pimp at age 15. Instead, I was raised in a Christian home, went to college, regularly attended church, sang in the choir, had respectable summer jobs. But look at me. Here I am right in the middle of this living hell.*

It was horrible. If people were watching a girl from the "hood"* "catching a beat down"† by a pimp or drug dealer, they wouldn't be able to tell the difference between that and my situation. The more I thought about it, the angrier I got. I crawled to the top of the stairs and said to Yari, "I'm leaving!"

Pointing in my face and angrily clenching his teeth, he ordered, "Get out! I want you out of here by the time I get back!" Something happened when he said that. Flying into a rage, I attacked him. I jumped on him, kneed him in the groin, and punched him in the face. Picking me up, he body-slammed me against the refrigerator. I gave up. My head and back were bruised and my finger was broken, but even worse, my pride was injured. All of that just because I had had sex. People don't realize that every decision they make has consequences. The problem was not that I was living with a lunatic, but that 12 years earlier I had made some decisions that landed me there in that kitchen.

§ § §

Let's go back to the beginning and you'll see just how I ended up in that situation.

I come from a large, very religious family (both of my parents were staunch Christians and active in the church). As the baby girl I felt lots of pressure to improve on all of the things that my older siblings had messed up. It was as if I were my parents' last hope.

I sensed the pressure in my teen years, but by the time I started college I really felt it. By then two of my sisters had had children out of wedlock, as had three of my brothers. So the stakes were high. Actually, my younger brother was only 10, so it was as if 5 out of 8 had already blown it. Interestingly enough, we were never in the dark about sex. We girls had the book *On Becoming a Woman,* read it, and asked our mother questions. Although Mom was a little shy, she would always answer honestly. Our family was very open—we talked about everything. That could have been because of my parents' experience.

My mother determined that we girls would do better than she had. Not that she was unhappy and didn't love my father, but she had married him when she was very young and she obviously didn't have a lot of dating experience. She married at 15 and had her first child at 16, so she really grew up overnight. Because of that my mother wanted us to date and have fun and enjoy our teenage years and not get married right away.

Although my mother did encourage me to date, she pounded into my head that I was not to have sex before I married. She always said, "You don't want to do that." And I just didn't want to disappoint her. In all honesty, during the early years my decision to wait until marriage had more to do with my mother than with the Lord. However, as I grew older my reason for saving myself for marriage took on more of a commitment to God. Of course, the moment you commit yourself to serve God, the devil has a trap waiting, and that was certainly my case.

I first started dating Yari when I was 15, and he pressured me to have sex with him from the very beginning of our relationship. Since I was determined not to have sex, the issue became how far I could go without having sex. And believe me, I had some very close calls.

They started about two weeks after we began dating. Since he was my first real boyfriend, I didn't know a lot. And what I did know I ignored. It was easier to act that way to give myself a little more freedom. So we quickly became involved in some very heavy petting. I would instruct him, "You can do this, but you can't do that." It was ridiculous. We would be naked in the bed but "technically" not having sex. One time I was naked in his bed and my sister stopped by his house (obviously his parents weren't at home). I jumped up and ran into the bathroom, but couldn't get my clothes on quickly enough.

When my sister knocked on the door, I told her that I was going to the bathroom and couldn't reach the door. As she was leaving she must have glanced into the bedroom (the bed was quite disheveled), because she went straight home and told my mother that I was having sex with Yari. The sad thing about the incident was that I was really upset with my sister for stopping by when I should have been grateful that she had interrupted us. But sex and related activities have a way of controlling your mind until you don't think rationally.

And speaking of irrational thinking, we once came so close to having sex that I really thought that I was going to get pregnant. I remember asking a nurse that if the penis was near the vagina and the man ejaculated, could a woman get pregnant? I also wanted to know how far sperm can travel before they die. The questions tell the story. I was out of control and scared to death. There were too many close calls.

To compound the problem, his family wasn't Christian. I don't ever recall seeing a Bible in their house. So he really didn't understand or appreciate my determination to wait. His family members thought that we were having sex and didn't object. Each of us saw things from two drastically different sets of family values, and it was so much easier for him to pull me down than for me to lift him up.

Keep in mind that through all the close calls I was living in a Christian home and attending church on a regular basis. But I heard a story once that explains my dilemma. A young woman discussed marrying a non-Christian with her pastor. The minister listened carefully, then told her to climb up on his desk and stand there. She looked at him strangely, but got up on the desk. Then he asked her to pull him up on the desk. But no matter how she tried, she couldn't.

"OK, let me help you down," he said next. In a matter of seconds she was down on the floor beside the pastor. The pastor had made his point. It is very easy to go down but extremely difficult to pull someone up. There was no way that I was going to pull Yari up. Too many forces were against it, including the fact that he was irreligious and felt no guilt whatsoever for being sexually active.

Plus, I was really of the "How far can I go?" and "How much can I do?" mind-set. I remember reading the back of a tampon box. It had several questions and answers that new users of the product might have. One caught my attention. "Can you lose your virginity by using tampons?" And I remember thinking, *Ah-ha, there's a loophole. If I can lose my virginity by using tampons I might as well go for it.* Of course, I ignored the manufacturer's reply that stated that you can't lose your virginity using a tampon.

At times I thought to myself, *Forget it; I'm going to go ahead and do this.* But then I would hear my mother's voice inside my head: "I know you and Yari really like each other. Don't mess up. Be careful." It was always enough to make me change my mind. My mother was a saint of sorts. Seeing her face and hearing her voice at those moments was the only thing that stopped me.

The close calls got more and more frequent until he finally broke up with me, because I wouldn't have sex with him. But not before he tried a couple other tactics to persuade me. The one that stands out most in my mind is the time he told me, "Your mother knows that you're going to do it." And then he added, "I talked to your father, and he told me just make sure I don't get you pregnant." I didn't believe that my mother expected me to have sex with him. Nor did I accept what he said about my father. But even though we were an open family I just didn't feel comfortable asking my father if he had actually said such a thing to Yari.

I suppose that it was a blessing that Yari broke up with me, because I know that had we stayed together I would have eventually given in. Each time my resistance became a little weaker. He had no reason to wait, since he was already sexually active and there were plenty of girls willing to have sex with him. We did get back together a time or two, and it was always the same. I would go as far as I could do without "technically" having sex.

Finally, we split up for good. I went off to a Christian college, got baptized again, and started all over. Then I returned home for a break only to fall right back into the same trap (Satan is quite persistent!).

§ § §

Eventually, I met another guy and got married. I was proud of myself since I was "technically" still a virgin. After all of the stress and strain of holding out I felt excited about legally having sex with my husband. But a most interesting (and rather sad) thing happened. My prior sexual relationships raised their heads in unexpected ways. No, I hadn't had intercourse with any of my boyfriends, but I had certainly been involved in sexual relationships. Deep kissing, touching, and being in bed naked definitely qualify as sexual behavior. I had stopped only at actual intercourse. Although I had never dated lots of guys, I had gone too far!

When you are in a sexual relationship and you feel the guilt afterward, a lot of times you think, *I should have gone all the way. After all, God knows what was in my mind, and I was so close anyway.* Then the pendulum swings the other way, and you find yourself crying out to God, "I was wrong; forgive me." If you do that for long enough (in my case years), by the time you enter marriage and have legitimate sex, you still feel guilty. It is almost habitual to feel guilty. For example, if every time you drink a cup of coffee you have a donut, eventually when you have a cup of coffee without a donut it doesn't feel right. So, by the time I was married and could have sex without guilt, I couldn't have sex without guilt.

That same gut instinct of fear and the feeling that I was doing something wrong was still there. I couldn't get rid of it. Every time we had any type of romantic interlude that led to physical expression, afterward I would feel sick and guilty. An underlying guilt pervaded everything—even though I had no reason to feel guilty. I had come to associate certain actions as wrong, and now couldn't shake the feeling. Never in my wildest dreams would I have imagined or anticipated that, but I have talked with others who have had the same experience.

My life wasn't going as I had planned, and my marriage ultimately ended in divorce. Right around that same time my mother—my moral compass—died suddenly. Alone and thousands of miles away from my family, I slid into depression, then decided to move back home. There I could grieve the simultaneous deaths of my mother and my marriage with the support of my family.

And there Satan had a trap waiting for me. His name was Yari (amazing how Satan keeps showing up with the very same temptation!). Both of us were getting out of bad relationships and were supposedly just friends. We started going to the movies and hanging out together. As I dealt with the grief from the sudden death of my mother and as I tried to make my family and friends think I was OK, he was there. But it was different with Yari—with him I didn't have to be superwoman. With Yari, I could just weep and sob and be broken. He was always consoling, kind, and sensitive. Then he started pressuring me to have sex. This time he said there was nothing in the way. I had been married and was no longer a virgin, and we were both adults free to make our own decisions. And I did just that. I made a conscious decision to have postmarital (I had been married), premarital (I wasn't married at the time) sex with him.

In one way I did make a conscious decision, but in

other ways I refused to think about the implications of what I was doing. When he actually penetrated the first time it startled me, and I thought in horror, *I am having sex with this man that I am not married to. The very same guy that I said no to 12 years before.* I couldn't believe that I actually had had real sex outside of marriage. The experience was devastating.

I had gone full circle. Yari and I had dated and I had said no; I got married, then divorced, and now I was having sex with him. But instead of recognizing my sin and getting out, I elected to go deeper. "Since you did it once," I said to myself, "why stop now?" It reached the point where I began initiating sex. At the time I was living at home with my family and would sneak out late at night and return early in the morning. I would let the car coast in or out of the driveway so that my family wouldn't hear the motor running. (Yes, I was an adult, but remember, people thought of us as a respectable Christian family.) I would say goodnight to my family, put my pajamas on, and get into the bed. Once everyone else went to bed I would sneak out of the house, go to Yari's place, and stay until the wee hours of the morning.

Never once did I consider using birth control, because that would have been an open admission to myself that I was having premeditated sex—and that to me constituted more sin than just happening upon sex. Of course, everybody knows sex doesn't just happen. A close friend who was single, sexually active, and on birth control (and also considered herself a Christian) convinced me that I was being stupid and needed to use some form of birth control. So I decided to start taking the pill. But the very week that I was to begin, I found out that I was pregnant.

I was out of town when I realized that I was pregnant. Of course news of such magnitude couldn't wait, so I called Yari and told him that I was pregnant and getting an abortion. (See how one sin leads to more and more sin?) It was just too much. My mother had just died, and my family was already stressed. It would have been too much for them to handle. "Why are you doing that?" Yari asked. When he suggested that we should get married, I agreed. We got engaged, but the relationship began to fall apart almost immediately. He wanted me to move in with him, and I wouldn't. I did have some pride and traces of my Christian upbringing left.

Ultimately, he cheated on me. Instead of dumping him when I found out, I moved in with him. I didn't want to, but I felt as if I were losing everyone I cared about. My mother had just died. Divorce had left me feeling inadequate and ugly, and my family was still shocked about the pregnancy. When Yari had originally asked me to move in I had refused, so he had started seeing the other girl. Now I rationalized that if I lived with him he would straighten up. One day, in desperation, I just packed my bags and went to his place. That is another consequence of premarital sex. It was just one compromise after another.

It is like putting your foot in lukewarm water and then adding more and more scalding water. When you do it that way, the pain is gradual and you develop a higher threshold for it. Eventually you get to the point that you can't tolerate it any longer. But it takes a lot longer. Meanwhile, Yari dumped the other girl, which should have been a signal for me. If a guy will drop another person for you, know that he will discard you for someone else. But at the time I was just flattered that he had picked me over her.

My happiness didn't last for long. I found out the hard and embarrassing way that he was seeing someone else when he gave me an infection that I knew a man can get only from another woman. Things were not going well at all. Depressed and confused, I didn't want to admit that I had made a terrible mistake. So for a while I tried to make the best of it. That is what a sexual relationship does. It forces you to tolerate things that you wouldn't normally accept because of the bond that sex creates.

Neither Yari nor I had much in common. You have to be so careful whom you select as a life partner. Each of you have to be of like mind, of like faith. Otherwise somebody is bound to be taken advantage of, and it will most likely be the Christian. I decided, like the prodigal son, to leave Yari and return to my father's house. And there you have it. We are right back at the beginning of the story. As I searched for my suitcases, Yari and I got into a major fight, and that's how I wound up being slammed against a refrigerator.

His wrath was certainly a horrible consequence of all my wrong decisions. People may think to themselves, *My boyfriend will never hit me, so I don't have to worry.* That may or may not be true, but there are other consequences as well. Let's look at some of them.

I had the baby alone. Instead of a husband to coach my breathing and hold my hand, my sisters had to fill in. They shared my pain and my joy, but I still felt alone. Yari should have been there.

Now I am a single parent, raising a child whose father could care less about her. He once told me, "If she is dying, leave a message on my answering machine." The consequences affect not only you but your potential children. And now my child has to suffer because I had a relationship with a man who wasn't worth it. Pregnancy is probably the most obvious consequence of an extramarital relationship. Unfortunately, there are more.

§ § §

Just for a moment I want to consider the "How far can I go?" question, because I know that there are countless young people just like me who want to get away with as much as they can without actually "doing it." Going too far is anything that spells compromise. It could be being fully clothed with someone's hand in your blouse (or pants). That is too far. Because that leads to something deeper. Any step beyond kissing and hugging is too far (and even that may be too far for some). Sex is a gradual thing. In most cases you build up to it. Most dating relationships are a gradual progression. You have to tell yourself, "Anything that makes me want more, is too far."

As I look back I realize now that the things that I did during my teen years really heightened my sexual awareness to the degree that it became a struggle not to want that type of interaction in every relationship. As I said earlier, when I finally did get married, all of those close calls that I had had, each of them involving so much guilt, kept playing in my mind. Even when I got into a legal relationship I had all of these hang-ups. It helped wreck my marriage. So anything that makes you want more sex outside of marriage is too far. Believe it or not, you may face even more consequences.

In addition to the pregnancy and the beating, I struggled with a feeling of being cheap. The odds are that probably you will never marry the person you are sexually involved with. It is just one more person whom you have allowed into your space with no real intentions for anything beyond a thrill. How good can you feel about that? You can't. And although I wasn't having vaginal sex with them, just the fact that someone's tongue is halfway down your throat trying to taste your tonsils or the fact that another person's hand is under your clothes will leave you feeling unclean. And that is a consequence. It is another issue that you have to deal with, something else to work through. And we haven't even touched on the spiritual aspects of the thing.

I have already mentioned that I was rebaptized. What I didn't say earlier was that I felt so guilty during the altar call that I was weeping and sobbing uncontrollably. I can't even explain how horrible I felt. Angry, guilty, remorseful, and sick about the whole thing, I just knew that I needed to start all over with God. The knowledge that you can ask for forgiveness with the confidence that God does forgive is an awesome feeling. He does forgive and cast your sins into the depths of the sea—but your deed is done. Just as you can't unring a bell, you can't undo the consequences of your actions. Can I undo my pregnancy? No! Can I reverse the situation and not have an incurable venereal disease? No! And you know what? The medicine currently costs me about $300 for 100 pills (and that lasts only two months). So I am looking at $1,800 per year for medicine alone. (How's that for a practical consequence?) Plus—and I know it sounds funny—but I sometimes think, *Andrea, think about what you made your guardian angel have to look at.* It was tawdry and dirty, and my guardian angel saw it all.

When you find yourself beginning a sexual relationship, you need to jump to the end of the story and look at it honestly. Don't focus on the present. Things for the moment may appear pretty nice. Instead, go all the way to the end and consider how your present actions will impact your future. Ask yourself, What is this relationship going to do to or for me in the long run? And not necessarily only from a spiritual perspective. The spiritual is vital, but a lot of times we blank out the spiritual altogether because we just can't deal with it. Sometimes you have to think about it from the practical and social perspectives.

The spiritual aspect immediately tells you that you are wrong. Oddly enough, people can cope with the spiritual issues more than the social rejection, because they know that God will forgive them. Although the spiritual part was tough for me, I knew (as evidenced by my rebaptism) that I could go back to God. I realized that He is faithful to forgive. But I still have a child and a venereal disease. And neither of those results is going to change. So your best bet is to know God loves you, and if you can let His love for you and your love for Him be enough to stop you from engaging in sexual activities, wonderful. But if you are like me, you will probably push the religious aspect aside. If that is the case, think about the lifelong consequences of your actions.

Admittedly, it is much more difficult to start all over once you have experienced sex. The Bible says: "Resist the devil, and he will flee from you" (James 4:7, KJV). The biggest problem is resisting. He will flee every time—if you have enough strength to resist in the first place. What you have to do is surrender completely to God, because you *don't* have the strength to do it on your own. The whole text actually says: "Submit yourselves therefore to God. Resist the devil, and he will flee from you." You and I must daily submit to God. I struggle with that, because, in all honesty, I would love to have sex. But I tell myself that we are getting really close to the end of time. "Andrea, you recovered the last time, but will you this time?" I think, *What if I were to die in the midst of my sin?*

It's a bad feeling and a bad place to be. A wrong sexual relationship brings no real joy, because guilt always lurks in the back of your mind. It keeps telling you that you are wrong, you are tainted, you are tarnished, you are unclean, you are unfit. Do whatever you have to escape the relationship. Talk to someone who can give you solid advice. Be honest with yourself and tell the person you are involved with that you can no longer do it even though you want to. Acknowledge the reality that both of you can be eternally lost just for literally seconds of pleasure. Even if it is the best 15 seconds of your life, it could be the 15 seconds that cause your physical and spiritual death. Sex is not worth eternal death.

I thank God that He turned me around. It was a gradual process with several different stages. First I prayed and began to feel accepted and embraced by God, but I was still being disobedient to His Word because I was living with Yari. I didn't yet fully trust God to handle my situation. At that time I hoped that Yari would see my relationship with God, that it would rub off on him, and that ultimately he would accept Christ. That was wrong. You can't win a person to Christ by compromising your standards.

I was living in sin while trying to prove to Yari that God's way is best. I should have left that to God. Interestingly enough, though, during the time that I was living with Yari my relationship with God did grow stronger. I think part of the reason was because so many times I felt I had nowhere else to turn. After I moved out and had the baby I felt totally broken. And when you are shattered to the core, only God can put you back together. And He healed me through people who prayed for me and encouraged me. People who never made me feel guilty. The worse thing you can do is to overwhelm people with guilt. They will feel that if everyone thinks bad of them, then they might as well just keep doing what they have been. But if you will embrace them in love, you will give them a desire to please God.

A big turning point for me was the birth of my daughter. I sensed a strong responsibility for her spirituality. "God," I said, "I have got to get right with You (for real), because I have to be a true example to my child." That was when I really started to read and study the Word of God. It encouraged me and changed my life. Sure, there have been times when I felt as if I was going to mess up, or give up living the godly life, but I keep reminding myself—no, the Holy Spirit keeps reminding— "Andrea, you are better than that, and you don't want to make mistakes of that magnitude again. So don't even look to the left or the right. Just keep your eyes on Me."

Sometimes we don't fully turn our backs on God—we just turn our faces away from Him. Scripture reminds us: "And thine ears shall hear a word behind thee, saying, This is the way, walk ye in it, when ye turn to the right hand, and when ye turn to the left" (Isa. 30:21, KJV). But I don't want to hear the voice from behind me—I want to hear it speaking from in front of me or beside me. If the voice speaks from behind me, that means my back is to God. For those who have drifted off course and are seeking God's guidance again, He says that they will hear

Him from behind. I want His voice to come from the front or the side, indicating that God is leading or walking right beside me. That is the position I want to be in with the Lord.

That doesn't mean that I haven't made mistakes or that I won't make more. Rather, it indicates that I recognize the power that I have through God and now know what the Bible is telling us when it declares: "Walk in the Spirit, and ye shall not fulfil the lust of the flesh" (Gal. 5:16, KJV). I am involved in a spiritual battle. And the only thing that can suppress the drives of the flesh is the Spirit of God. So instead of praying, "Lord, help me to avoid this situation. Help me not to have sex. Help me not to get into a near miss situation. Help me not to have any close calls" we should be praying, "God, fill me with Your Spirit. Let Your Holy Spirit be in complete control." Our prayer should be: "Let this mind be in [me], which was also in Christ Jesus" (Phil. 2:5, KJV), because Jesus' mind focused on doing the will of His Father. We have to admit: "Lord, on my own I can't do it." To paraphrase Paul, "The good that I should do I ain't tryin' to do," but in the Spirit I praise God that I can do all things, including remaining pure till I marry or until Jesus comes!

---

* Slang term for bad neighborhood
† Slang term meaning to be beat up

All That Glitters Is Not Gold

Sarah's Story

Do you get your information about sex from magazines?
Do you find yourself sneaking out to have dates, because your parents are too strict?
Do you think you know a lot about sex?
The bottom line is "What Would Jesus Do!"
Sarah's is a story of victory. Read it for yourself.

Raised in a very strict, religious home
Mixed Hispanic/Anglo heritage
One sibling

I'm 16 years old and have a brother. We are originally from the Southeast. The members of my family basically keep to themselves, and we don't talk about deep stuff unless there's a big problem. When it comes to me dating, my family is quite conservative, though I guess we are pretty open-minded otherwise.

Here is how the dating situation recently played out in my family. I was interested in a guy who was an 18-year-old college freshman. We wanted to go on a date. My dad said no, because—and I quote—"You're only 16." It bothers me that I am going to be a senior next year and still don't have the freedom to date. It looks as if I'm not going to have it until I'm away at college. I feel that there is *no* way that I'll be able to have a boyfriend that I can feel comfortable with in front of adults until I am at college and totally independent of my parents. I would never dare hold hands with a guy in front of them now. They make it so uncomfortable that I have to sneak around to date.

One guy in particular, named Mike, they really didn't like. My parents had no clue that I went with him for two years. They didn't want me to talk to him, because he belonged to a different religion. Also they thought that he was a "sex freak" and that he would hurt me or something.

I think they are so nervous about me having a boyfriend because they fear I already know too much about guys and stuff. My parents worry that I will grow up too early. Mom is of Hispanic background and was raised very strictly in the church. She didn't have a boyfriend until she was in college, never kissed anyone but my dad, and was *very* reserved. But I am totally different.

In a way, I do know a lot for a 16-year-old. But I didn't realize it until I was talking to one of my friends who is away at college. He is my best friend, and I can talk to him about anything! I told him about some of my past experiences. Actually, I was feeling rather guilty about something that I had done and was having a hard time getting over it. "Sarah, I would have never guessed that you know about that stuff at your age," he said afterward, "much less *do* it!"

Anyway, I have basically learned about sex by reading magazines (not the porno ones, just *Cosmo* and *Mademoiselle*). Also I have older friends that talk about sex and stuff. As a result I've gone from going "um . . . huh?" in a conversation to understanding and contributing to the jokes. I've also picked up some stuff from movies and songs and music videos. My parents and I don't talk about sex, however, which is fine with me. It would be too embarrassing for them, and I don't want to hear it from them at this point. I know enough about it anyway—I could give myself "the talk."

Now, let me say that I haven't had sex and don't plan to. I have decided to wait until I am married—*but* that was only after a very close call. One boyfriend and I were really "touchy-feely" all the time—it is embarrassing to talk about. He and I were making out in his room, and he wanted to go all the way. For a moment I also wanted to, but suddenly I thought about God and what He wants me to do, then I considered the man whom I'll marry in the future and realized that I wanted to save that gift for him. I didn't want to be ashamed on my wedding night by having to say, "Dear, there have been many more men in my past. You're not the first one I've slept with."

Another thing that stopped me after all these thoughts went through my mind was the fact that we had been swimming earlier and were still in our bathing suits, so it wasn't very convenient. Taking advantage of that, I jumped off the bed. Then I told him that it was wrong, and that if he loved me, he wouldn't ever ask me to do something like that again. But if he did ask, I would tell an adult, and he would be in trouble. He started crying and said, "Sarah, you know I love you . . . I'm sorry, sweetie. Please forgive me." And stupid me, I forgave him. Later I learned that he was a sex maniac and that he made out with other girls when he and I weren't together. Besides that, he drank and stuff. Gross. His appearance was attractive, but he was totally unattractive when it comes to personality. And yes, it was the very same guy that my parents were worried about.

Since that experience I have had only one boyfriend.

It is hard for me to get close to guys, both emotionally and physically. In fact, I can't seem to get close to anyone. Even with the boyfriend I currently have I only recently kissed him, and that was hard enough, because I kept thinking about Mike. The experience had made me feel like trash, as if I had been violated and exposed too much of myself. Now it is hard to get close to guys, because I know that what I did with Mike was wrong—and just the thought of doing that stuff again hurts me terribly. It was a horrible experience, one that I don't ever want to go through again. I'm sorry, I can't talk about it anymore—I have to go. I hope this helps someone.

When You Play With Fire You Will Get Burned!
Bryan's Story

If you think of sex as a game
If you think that pregnancy is the only consequence of premarital sex
If you think that guys don't have to deal with consequences too, read
*   Bryan's story.*
A sexual pyromaniac, Bryan started at a very young age, is now married
*   with children, and is still dealing with the consequences of "playing*
*   with fire."*

Male
32 years old
"Military Brat"
Attended a Christian college
Raised as a Christian in a two-parent upper-middle-class home.

We are sitting in the guest room of Bryan's very nice home. The door is shut, but we can still hear the children playing. It is obvious that it is a Christian home.

Bryan, thanks for agreeing to this interview. Let's get right down to business. Tell me about your first sexual experience.

I had it at age 11. I was relaxing and talking in a sauna with my buddy when two teenage girls came in. They asked us if we wanted to play "Chicken." Neither of us knew what it was, but we didn't want to look dumb so we just said yes. The girls decided that they would go first. So the first girl walked up to me and started at my ankles and said "Chicken?" When I said no, she moved up a little higher—calves, knees, thighs. Eventually she touched my penis. I said yes. So she stopped and we switched partners. The other girl started at my ankles. "Chicken?" And of course, I responded no. When she reached my penis and said "Chicken?" I still answered no.

Now it was my turn to see if she was "Chicken." One thing led to another, and the next thing we knew clothes started coming off. I was young and really didn't know what I was doing. I ended up just lying on top of her for a little while. Then I saw my older and more experienced friend out of the corner of my eye and imitated what he did. Before I knew it I was inside of the girl, and we were having sex in the sauna. Believe it or not, we didn't get caught, which was strange because it was generally a pretty busy place. After that I started to have sexual sensations. It is amazing how just one experience can start a whole train of events. It was a thrill—almost like a roller-coaster ride to some degree.

Did your parents talk to you about sex?

I gleaned all of my sexual knowledge from the streets, the basketball court, and the other guys. My parents were young, and I don't think they really knew what to say. I think my dad assumed that since I was just a kid, they should just let me keep thinking about childish things. By the time my father discussed sex with me I was already sexually active. But I didn't tell him. I enjoyed sex, but it felt wrong. I felt dirty when I was around my parents. But I started to indulge more and more.

Before the sauna experience did you know that you would,

at some point prior to marriage, have sex?

Yeah, I did. I guess it was because I watched what people did on TV, in the movies, and in magazines. Everything I saw had a sexual connotation to it. To me, it was the thing to do. Even though it was a bad thing, it still seemed the thing to do. In other words, people made you believe that sex was bad, but I felt that it wasn't so much that it was bad as it was just being hidden from me. I concluded that it was a hidden lifestyle, one permitted for adults, but something that I wasn't old enough to indulge in yet. The mystery made me extremely curious.

Discuss some of the consequences of what you did.

At 11 years of age I didn't think of getting someone pregnant. In fact, I hadn't even heard about birth control. Nor had I heard that much about sexually transmitted diseases. The only consequence that I thought of was getting caught, and I knew that I was smart enough to avoid that. There were too many places for me to do it and too many people who would watch my back.

As I think about it now, another consequence is that when you start having sex, it begins spreading rapidly through your mind like a disease. You want it more and more. Nor does it end with one person. You start craving it with other people. Once you start dating it is difficult to have a relationship that is free of sex. You begin with kissing and touching, then it goes to heavy petting. From there it's actual intercourse. As I got older it was tough to determine whether I really loved the girl for who she was or if it was the pleasure of the sex. Then as an adult I didn't care whether it hurt the woman or not. It was a matter of me getting my satisfaction. I would tell her that I loved her, but when we reached a certain point, it was all about me. I would say, "Just lie there for a few minutes; I can help you enjoy this." I would say anything at that time to get what I wanted. That was the key. To be able to get what I wanted when I wanted it.

OK, at age 11 consequences were not an issue. At what point did you begin to think about them?

(Bryan smiles strangely.) When I was about 16 I started seriously dating a girl that, because of a medical condition, couldn't get pregnant. *(Now I understand the smirk.)* I was in my heyday! Just at the time that I would have really begun to focus on consequences, Satan provided a situation that freed me from the one result that I would have been concerned about—pregnancy. But I started to think about the other consequences when I found out that she was interested in another guy. Eventually, it came out that she was having sex with him. At the same time I became aware of sexually transmitted diseases and realized that maybe I needed to be a little more careful. I thought about it and talked about it, but didn't always take the necessary precautions. Right after we broke up she acquired a sexually transmitted disease. It was a close call and should have been a wake-up call, but it wasn't.

During my junior year in college I dated four girls at one time and had sex with three of them. All three of them ended up on the campus during the same weekend. I spent so much energy trying to have sex with all of them and yet keep them apart that I actually collapsed on the football field and had to be rushed to the hospital. I was hyperventilating, and according to the emergency room personnel, actually came close to death.

Not long after that experience, I finally decided to

become a one-woman man. I was seeing a young woman who was very attractive and kind of mysterious in a way. She had a child, seemed to be very mature, and knew what she wanted out of life. Our relationship progressed and was getting pretty serious in that we discussed marriage and her child being my stepson, etc. As a result we became sexually active. It reached the point that every time we saw each other it involved sex. Eventually, we got so engrossed that we stopped taking precautions. Caught up in a romantic fantasy world of sorts, we felt that it was just the two of us and the two of us alone. Well, she ended up getting pregnant.

I was somewhat excited, because I felt that I really loved her and was prepared to do the right thing to raise our child. However, she didn't have the same idea. She ended up having an abortion. It wasn't my choice, but she was firm. Although she wouldn't let me go with her to the clinic, I did have to pay for it. One of the most hurtful parts of the situation was that she never made me a part of the decision process. After she decided that she was having an abortion, that was that. I felt as if my manhood was being threatened. In addition, we broke up and she moved to another state. And to add salt to the wound, one of the last things she told me was that she had thought that she loved me, but she really didn't. I was so hurt that I was angry—angry with God, my parents, and myself.

Up to this point I had deluded myself that my sexual involvement had been "clean." No pregnancy. No diseases. No problems. And now Satan had trapped me, and the dirt was finally coming out. You don't think about it at the time, because it [the baby] isn't even here yet. But later I knew that I couldn't fool myself any longer. I had actually allowed a life to be taken. And I felt fear, because the girl I loved could have died on that table. All this turmoil and stress for 5 minutes of pleasure. It caused me to look back and to see that premarital sex does have serious consequences. Not only is there potential for a child to be born, but it also made me realize that abortion and childbirth can put the mother at serious risk as well. That experience left me hurting.

Depressed because of some other situations in my life, I attended a revival held at school. My best friend introduced me to a young woman I'll call Marsha. She and I attended the revival, and we both decided to get baptized and give our lives to Christ. We also started dating. On a spiritual high, I felt good about myself and was confident that my sexual escapades were over. In retrospect, I realize that there was a point that I became worried that I was addicted to sex, that I was some sort of sex maniac. It was with a sense of relief that things were different with Marsha. We talked, read the Bible, and prayed together. At most we held hands and kissed—that was it. I really enjoyed the relationship and the freedom from the sexual issues that had plagued me.

But one night we were alone, and as we kissed, our hands started moving, and before we knew it we had sex. The second fall is always worse than the first. This relationship became ridiculous in terms of sex. We would have it *anywhere.* From outside on a picnic bench or the ground, to inside in classrooms—wherever. She would wear "easy access" clothing, and I would take advantage of it. Our spiritual relationship turned 180 degrees and became nothing but a sexual relationship. We had given Satan full rein in our lives, and I hated it. It was the first time in my life that I had encountered a woman so aggressive with regard to sex. Realizing that I wanted more out of a relationship, I broke up with her. Hindsight tells me that Satan had handpicked Marsha for me. He knew that I was serious about my commitment to God, but not strong enough to say no to a woman's advances. In addition, I wasn't praying and studying God's Word as I had at the beginning—another lesson learned the hard way.

After I escaped that relationship, I chilled out for a while, but eventually I met and started dating Tami. She was a virgin, and I was glad. Tami was the perfect girl, and I knew that sex wouldn't be an issue. We did a lot of fun things together. Our relationship was such that we could go to our friend's apartment, sleep on the floor side by side, and nothing would happen. We didn't expect anything to happen. My mind was finally free. At last I had found the girl that I didn't want to make love to until after we said "I do." I told her that and promised her that I was going to marry her. We were looking forward to a life together.

Eventually I visited her parents' home, and I'm not lying when I tell you that Satan himself came along for the ride. We listened to a religious radio program and had a nice conversation with her father. When the program went off, he went to bed. His bedroom and mine were connected. I pulled out the sofa bed and got ready to crash. Then I heard a knock on the other door that led into the room where I was to sleep. When I opened the door there stood my virgin girlfriend in a see-through nightgown! It took me by surprise. I asked her what she was doing. She said that she was there to kiss me goodnight. The kiss led to more and more. Soon we lost control, and right there, with her father in the very next room, we had sex. The girl lost her virginity and I lost my self-respect and felt that I had destroyed her.

Shortly before that night I had begun to sense a growing doubt about the whole relationship. I had begun wondering whether she was really the one, but after we had sex I had to keep up a lie. So I kept telling her that we were going to get married. I did love her, but wasn't sure if I wanted to spend the rest of my life with her. After we had sex the first time, I wanted to have it with her all the time. For a long time I thought as a man that it was a big thing to be a woman's first sexual partner. It seemed great that whatever I told her about sex was the gospel in her mind. We were doing just about everything, but I started to feel really bad that I was the one to teach her. I felt like a parent instructing his child in the lies and evils of the world. Our relationship became just like all the others. It was purely a sexual relationship.

By now I was thoroughly sick and tired of the cycle, and in this case, I knew that I had really crushed a person's hopes. I had almost acquired a sexually transmitted disease, I couldn't or wouldn't control my sexual desires, I had caused the death of an innocent child, and I had taken a woman's virginity. It had shaped up to be an extremely ugly picture. Eventually, the girl and I broke up. It just wasn't working out. We never really talked about all of the reasons why we separated, and I felt guilty for years. Of course people who knew about the situation constantly reminded me of what a dog I had been as well. As I grow and learn I realize how much I was wrong. However, I can also say that we were both adults and responsible for our actions. It was the second time in a row that Satan had brought temptation to me, instead of me going after it. And for the second time I fell for it.

After I ended that relationship I started spending time with my best friend, one of my greatest inspirations. She had always been a special person to me. We had been together all through college, but just hadn't dated. I think God had kept us apart because He knew my life and didn't want her to become a part of that tangled web. The young woman was as a sister to me. It was strange—whatever she wanted, I gave her. I had a decent job by this time and was happy to spoil her. Although we were close, our relationship had nothing physical about it.

One day as we rode together down the street I realized that I had begun to like her as more than a sister. It was most confusing and just didn't seem right. She felt like family. I kept looking at her and then reached over and kissed her—and she slapped me! *(A big grin stretches across Bryan's face.)* I will never forget that day. I don't know what I expected, but it wasn't a slap. When I asked her why she slapped me, she stopped the car and said, "Because I didn't know how to react." By the end of that night we were kissing again. We started to date and had lots of fun together. I felt very comfortable with her, because we had been friends for so long. As our relationship progressed, I wanted to take her out for a special evening and do it up right.

We had a wonderful time. Afterward she decided to spend the night, since my parents were out of town. Now, the interesting thing here is that she wanted to take birth control (just in case), and I was against it. Because we were "unprotected" she told me not to come inside of her, but I did. That very same night both of us had a feeling that she was going to get pregnant. I felt badly because I realized that I had again let Satan get the best of me. I was sure that she was the one for me—that God had ordained our relationship, yet I had allowed Satan to mess me up.

Well, as it turned out she was pregnant. Since we had been planning to get married anyway, we just moved the date up a few months. We were sorry that she was pregnant and also that we had had sex. Both of us had a profound belief that our relationship was part of God's plan. We got baptized together and started our new (and very stressful) life. Our first child entered the world six months after our wedding.

We missed a lot of the early part of our marriage, because we had to focus on our new baby. I was still somewhat immature, and it was difficult. At times I wondered if we would make it. I can tell you that it was her relationship with God that kept us together in the early days. I know that had it been completely up to me I would have messed up again. Although I loved her, I wasn't ready for marriage. I thank God for her. We have been married for 10 years now and are deeply in love.

Would you make the same decisions again?

No, I don't think I would. I was so sexually active prior to marriage that I was addicted to it—you can quote me on that. Young people don't understand the addictive power of sex. Like alcohol or drugs, it produces a high. I was on my way to a serious problem and didn't even realize it. I wanted books, magazines, movies—whatever I could get my hands on that had to do with sex. After I watched the movies or had sex with the young women I felt dirty, much like that of the alcoholic or drug addict after a weekend of partying. It caused major self-esteem problems for me and reached the point where I thought of myself almost as a beast, craving only one thing—sexual pleasure. I desperately wanted to give it up, but I didn't know where to turn.

Although I tried to turn to the Lord, I never committed myself 100 percent to Him. I had never realized that it takes more than a one-day or one-week spiritual high to turn around what I had gotten into. No, I wouldn't make the same decisions again, because the consequences are too serious. You hurt people. When you break a person's trust you have nothing. It also destroys the marriage relationship, because the natural tendency is to compare your sexual partners. It is unfair to your spouse. The bottom line is that what the Bible says is true. God says *wait*. The Bible says abstain from fornication.

I know it is hard. It was hard back then, and the pressure is worse now. Don't throw your life away. A moment of pleasure has the potential to seriously impact, even destroy, three lives: an innocent child's, your partner's, and yours!

What will you tell your children about sex?

I want to tell my kids what my parents didn't tell me. I have explained to my son the facts about male and female anatomy. We have also talked about the consequences of premarital sex. He knows that sex is for married people. I feel it is my duty to be honest, and I have told him that I wasn't always the Christian that I am now. I hope that by being truthful, I will help him to become the Christian that God expects him to be.

The thing that frightens me most is my son coming to me and asking, "Dad, why didn't you tell me?" I know parents shy away from the subject of sex, but we can't afford to do that anymore. Too much lurks out there that can hurt our children. Technology makes it possible for our kids to be exposed to sex in the comfort of our own homes via computer. Some parents grew up in an age of sexual promiscuity that was, at least at the time, fun. Today, the same actions can have deadly results. We have to talk to our children about the whole issue.

The other thing I want my son to know is that I love him, and he can tell me anything. I would rather create an environment in which we can discuss things versus one that makes him ashamed or afraid to speak to me.

Bryan, what is your advice to young people making the same decision?

Don't do it! Leave premarital sex alone! I know it is hard. Satan is going to do everything he can to put you in a bad situation. If I could tell you to pick up the phone and call me every time you got in a tight spot, I would do that, but I know you won't call, because you don't want to. You want to be in such a situation. It sounds trite, but it's true. Pray and put God first and avoid situations that will lead to sex. I don't care how good it may seem; think of the consequences, then look at where you are. That way you will see the whole story.

You have your whole life in front of you. Having a sexual relationship doesn't make you more of a man or woman. That is an outright lie. I would challenge you to hold on to your love for yourself and God. To know that you can go home and look in the mirror and be happy about what you did that day. It is a sad feeling to return home hating yourself. Sin is fun—I'm not going to lie to you. But we know that the wages of sin is death. Somebody's going to die. Something's going to happen. I'm not trying to scare you into doing right, but just want to give you the real and the honest picture.

The Great Escape

Anri's Story

This is one of the most disturbing and at the same time one of the most triumphant stories you will find within the pages of this book.

It disturbs me, because I experienced a part of it, even though it isn't my story.

It is disturbing, because incest and abuse do exist within the church.

It is disturbing, because most of us are afraid to touch people with certain issues. And usually those are the people who need to be touched the most.

It is triumphant, because God took a broken spirited little girl and made her into a powerful and wonderful woman.

It is triumphant, because she refuses to hide from the pain of her past. She faces it, with God's help, and allows His healing power to transform her life.

It is triumphant, because despite so much potential for continued hurt and hate, she instead chooses love and acceptance.

It is triumphant, because she is allowing God to make her whole.

After starting this chapter for the eighth time (at least), I have decided to share the story with you just as I experienced it, through a number of e-mail messages that Anri and Gwen sent back and forth to each other. It is longer than the other chapters, but I believe the detail is necessary for you to understand the level of hurt and the level of healing that has taken place in Anri's life.

Trust me when I tell you that the mere fact that Anri's story is a part of this book is proof that it is God's will for it to be here. Perhaps if you have experienced sexual abuse, homosexual relationships, and/or promiscuity in heterosexual relationships, or if you just love a good story that shows God's awesome power, then Anri's process of restoration and healing will be as much of a blessing to you as it has been to me.

§ § §

Hey, Gwen, it has been great getting back in touch with you after all this time. I'd like to share something with you. I am a survivor of sexual abuse, and God has brought me a very, very long way. I love to tell people who I was and where I was just so they can see who God is and where He can lead them. God is faithful!

I grew up in a Christian home with five sisters and brothers and two hardworking parents. My dad began molesting me when I was about the age of 4 or 5. While other kids were playing and having fun, I was being sexually abused. Pain, sadness, and loneliness were my playmates. Confusion was my constant companion. From the very beginning I worked to earn and keep my nickname—Buddy. That was what my dad called me— Buddy. I tried to be his buddy, thinking that if I was good enough and quiet enough he wouldn't hurt me. But no matter what I did, he continued to hurt me.

The strange thing is that even though he abused me, I loved him. I knew it was wrong, but I wanted to protect him. But protection for him meant destruction for me. As I literally separated myself from the abuse by pretending that it wasn't happening, I began to destroy myself. Eventually I blocked out all memories of the abuse. Others abused me as well: a neighbor woman, my grandmother, my brother, a teenage boy, and a deacon in our church. For years I consciously blanked the abuse out. However, the resulting emotional trauma was always present.

As I grew, my playmates grew too. Pain matured into anger, sadness developed to bitterness, loneliness became isolation and withdrawal, and confusion remained my steady companion. And somewhere along the way, the pretend game became reality. I made it appear that I had it all together. I was the type of person that people aspired to be like. No job was too hard, and I could do it better and faster than anyone. I was invincible (on the outside). The funny thing was that the pretend game worked only on the outside. On the inside my heart was broken, and I hated being alone. Eventually my playmates began to take over my life and smother whatever semblance of me still remained. In the end it was my ever-present, constant companion—confusion—that struck the final blow, and I cried, "God, what is wrong with me?"

Little did I know the depth of that question. Had I known, I might not have asked it. But God mercifully, little by little, peeled my hands away from in front of my mind's eye. He allowed me to remember the abuses of my childhood and explained the reasons for my fear of being alone, my perfectionism, ulcers, mistrust of men, rebellion against authority figures, attraction to women, workaholism, food addiction, and inability to trust Him totally. Probably it is difficult for you to comprehend the weight of my burden. It is even more difficult for me to put it into words.

Wanting to trust God, I remembered that His Word said: "Come unto me." But that presented another problem, because I was angry at God—really angry. I needed to know where He had been when I was being abused. When I was a little girl going to church, trying to be the perfect little child, and being abused instead of embraced with love—where was He then? If He was supposed to be so big and powerful, how come He didn't protect me? I couldn't just read the Bible and trust it to be true because of these questions lurking in my mind. In time, though, God showed me Isaiah 63:9 that begins: "When they suffered, He [Jesus] suffered" (Clear Word). In time I came to understand that Jesus took the fatal blow, and I received only the glancing one. Slowly I understood that there really is comfort and peace in God.

§ § §

One of the most painful parts of my healing process came when, right in the middle of my personal pity party, God began to show me what I was like. As He patiently peeled my hands off of my mind's eye, He revealed to me a terrible truth. He said to me, "Daughter, you have sinned."

I almost couldn't believe what He was showing me. "How have I sinned?" I asked myself. "I have been the model church-going, tithe-paying, Bible study-giving, missionary-spirited woman all along!"

God indicated to me that my reactions to my abuse had been sinful. He showed me other sinful choices that I had made along the way—how I had reacted with anger, hatred, and rage. I had caused both Him and others a lot of pain. The ground at the foot of the cross is level, He reminded me. He had died not only for me but for both those who had wronged me and those whom I had wronged in turn. Gradually I realized that we must all go to Jesus, and that when we are at the cross I'm face-to-face with those who have harmed me. I *cannot* look down on them. Well, Gwen, there you have it. Through it all, I can see God working in my life.

§ § §

Anri, I am almost speechless (and you know that isn't normal). Let me start at the very beginning and take you through my reaction to your story. I received the package you sent as I was on my way out of the door to work. As I explore what I felt, I guess I knew that it would probably confirm what I had only suspected. I knew your story would be deep, and I also knew that reading it would make me wish that I could have been more supportive when you needed it. Also I figured that your account would answer some questions I've had through the years. But even more than having those questions answered, I was eager to read it, because when people get to a point that they are ready to share, it means that God is working and that healing is taking place. And I was so glad for you in that respect, Anri.

Because of some of the things you mentioned in other e-mails, I figured that your story would have something to do with abuse. But let me tell you what happened. When I started to read the story, all of a sudden I didn't want to know. I put it down. I'm not squeamish or one who believes that we shouldn't address certain topics. So, why my response? I don't know.

I did finally get the courage to read the story, and all I can say is: Praise God! You are right, He is faithful! Know that I am praising God with you!

Love,

Gwen

§ § §

Gwen, you mentioned your wish that you had been more supportive. You and Alisa were my friends. When I relate the story of "my great escape," I always tell people that you guys were my lookout. When it wasn't safe to live at home and I went there only to sleep, you or Alisa would call me and tell me when Sally was coming home. I never knew if you knew about our relationship. One thing I did know was that you cared about me, not about what I did.

You know, the problem of homosexuality is so prevalent in the church. At first, discussing it in public was difficult and shameful. But now, I share it regularly, because so many people struggle with the issue. Today, I am very proud of the road the Lord has taken me down. I am very thankful that He continued to lead me and guide me, even when I chose to lead myself. I have really talked to only one other person who has been a part of my past. I knew that she loved me too, but our relationship was quite different from mine and yours. She and I are still very good friends, but our hearts don't connect. I really need to talk to someone who was an eyewitness to that part of my life. I have never thought about that before, but as I type it rings so true in my heart. I think God has a deeper healing here for me.

As I continue to heal I recognize that injured people hurt other people and that there is a measure of defilement that needs to be dealt with. Defilement that you and Alisa encountered even though you may not have been aware of it. As a matter of fact, believe it or not, I didn't know the truth about Sally and me. I think maybe I was afraid to face it. I was in so much denial, but I needed to do that just to live. That's why talking about it will bring a different measure of healing—it already has. Thanks again, my friend. The connection for me has been heaven-sent.

Love,
Anri.

§ § §

Anri, we can certainly talk about this anytime you like. I find it very interesting that you say you didn't recognize the nature of the relationship between you and Sally. That could explain why you never told us. I am very interested in what your thought process was and what made you decide to make the "great escape." It seemed to be so sudden. I think it will be interesting for us to compare notes. My memories of you are not centered around what you did, but who you were.

I love you more,
Gwen

§ § §

Gwen, when I look back, I see that I was so controlled, foolish, and gullible. My relationship with Sally changed the day she held my hand, and I told her I was uncomfortable with it. She explained that was the way she expressed her affection as a friend, and if I wasn't comfortable with it, we couldn't be friends. Gwen, I was such a lonely, mixed-up girl. Sally was the only friend I'd ever had, and I wasn't about to do anything to mess that up. So I silenced my conscience, turned on the denial button (I was accustomed to doing that), and went along with her program.

When I say I didn't know the truth about us, I knew that I "loved" her and she "loved" me, and that love would cover a multitude of sins. I recognized that she made me feel good, and that my conscience made me feel bad. I sensed that what we were doing was wrong, but I had no label for it. But my need for love and acceptance outweighed my desire to do the right thing. Don't get me wrong, I wasn't the little victim being pulled along by a ring in my nose. I did a good bit of using myself—it was all so self-centered. She made me feel good, and that was something I'd never really had, but I paid a high price for it.

Eventually, I tired of the game. Trying to live two lives was exhausting. The other thing is that I really did like guys. Tim came into our lives at a most crucial point. Favoring neither me nor Sally, he was really "our" friend, but I was smitten by him. I think I was looking for a way out. All I wanted and needed was for someone to say to me, "Anri, it looks like you may be in some trouble. I love you, and anytime you want to talk about it or need help in getting out, I'm here for you." I longed for people to tell me that, but no one did. Everyone was too afraid to touch the issue.

The crisis between Sally and me came when I realized that I liked Tim and started visiting him alone. I think you and Alisa covered for me on that too. Sally found out, though, and we had several big blowups. She was extremely angry about it. I went into a few rages also. Once I went after her with a knife, because she was "slapping me around." (I use the term loosely, because she wasn't trying to hurt me. In fact, she wasn't hurting me,

but I was sick and tired of the control and manipulation.)
I couldn't think.

All I knew was that I needed to get out, and I acted on
impulse. It was all very sudden. Sometimes I was afraid
that Sally was possessed by the devil. However, the truth
is that both of us had put ourselves under his control.

Staying in that situation wasn't an option. Leaving
was my only choice, and I knew she wouldn't let me do
that. There was going to be a fight, and I had nothing to
battle her with. All I knew how to do was run. And run I
did. I was so afraid of her that I couldn't even live in the
house the final two weeks. I basically lived in my car and
slept at home only if I knew for sure that she wouldn't be
there. But you know, the story doesn't end there. Even
after I moved to another state she was still controlling
me, and I even paid her what I call "alimony" so she
could stay in the apartment. I paid off the furniture bill,
none of which I kept, I might add.

I wish I had known who I was back then. I had no idea.
I often wish I'd had the opportunity to redo those years as
a healthy, whole person. I think I would like that. I would
like to hear your perception of me then. Everything I did
was only in reaction to something else. I never stopped to
think things through. It was all very impulsive.

But there is more to the story. Although we were no
longer living together, I was, as I said, still under her control. I left in February, but Christmas of the same year
(10 months later) she was still visiting me. The physical
involvement had ceased at that point, but you understand that the emotional involvement comes first, lasts
longer, and has a stronger hold, which means it is more
difficult to sever. By then I was dating R.D., who is now
my husband. One day she showed up at my apartment

and went into a jealous rage with him, his friend, my roommate, and me. It was sickening! I think that was the last straw for me.

It was time to move on with my life (for real), but not before I did some explaining. That night I told R.D. the whole story. I admired him for understanding. Making no judgments, he still wanted to be with me. He accepted me, and acceptance was one of my greatest unmet needs. We married, had our first child a few years later, and my recovery began early in the 1990s.

§ § §

During the early part of the year I told myself that it was going to be my "Year of Truth." Little did I know the magnitude and depth of the truth I would encounter. I purchased a book for a friend called *The Promise of Restoration*. It was about childhood sexual abuse (which her child had unfortunately experienced). I read the book before sending it to her—not because I felt that I needed it, mind you. I just wanted to know what I was sending.

Well, as I read the book my chest started to hurt and I began hyperventilating. Something was drastically wrong. I completed a short survey that identified symptoms of those who had been abused. According to the survey, if you had even one of the major symptoms, there was a high probability that you had experienced some sexual abuse in your history. Gwen, I had nine of the major symptoms, same-sex relationships being one of them. In addition, I had many of the minor ones.

Floored by the implications, I began to ask God to show me the truth. The next day, after praying, I had my first flashback. It was of a neighbor woman molesting me. I was so afraid. Shortly after that I began having flashbacks about my dad. I called my two oldest sisters, and they confirmed that the woman had indeed molested me. They then told me what our father had done to them. No one had ever talked about it until I began. They said that they hadn't known that he had abused the younger ones. I had blocked most of my childhood memories, but now God mercifully returned them. I started looking for solutions. Counseling was one of them. I went to a Christian counselor, and that began my road to recovery.

Then I went to a women's retreat designed specifically for the sexually abused. The process they used for ministering was gentle, Bible-based, and loving. It encouraged me to look more at my feelings about the abuse and take responsibility for the choices I'd made as a result of the abuse. It also gave me a greater measure of healing than I had experienced through counseling. I could really see that God was in the process. As I looked where He was during the hellish circumstances and what He was doing now to rectify them, I could see Him guiding me.

The process the women's retreat introduced to me was gentle. It focused on restoring my broken relationship with God. We call the process "good grief." Although it can be painful and scary, knowing the truth about God makes one willing to walk through the "valley of the shadow of death."

I never tell people that I'm healed. Instead, I let them know that it is a process. We walk to the Promised Land together. I have been over some ground that they in turn must walk. Because I know where some of the potholes and sinkholes are, I can tell them what I encountered should they walk the same way. But they have also been to places that I have not been. Sharing brings about deeper healing, exposes areas that still need God's healing touch, and provides opportunity to reveal deep and beautiful truths about God.

Thank you for being willing to dialogue about this subject. If it were not for you, I don't know to whom I would have talked. May I quote Mordecai? "You may just have come to the kingdom for such a time as this." Thanks. I'm really serious. And I know I'm not done yet, so please keep asking questions. God knows that I heal quicker when I can get it out. The hardest part of this whole thing is to realize my vulnerability.

But I know His promise is true. God said that He would restore the years that the locusts have eaten. This exchange, my friend, is part of that restoration.

Love,
Anri

§ § §

When I close my eyes, I keep seeing your words: "All I wanted and needed was for someone to say to me, 'Anri, it looks like you may be in some trouble.'" That really speaks volumes. Sometimes I see people headed for trouble and make excuses not to get involved. By God's grace I will always let the power of your words and God's guidance at least push me to ask the question of others.

In a way I'm glad that I didn't actively recall all of those events. I think that our friendships are defined by our memories. For me, that means that I remembered the positive and didn't get bogged down in the other stuff, which I think is ultimately the reason that I can comfortably relive it, so to speak, now. It isn't as if I'm recalling some terribly horrifying experience.

I do remember one major event, however. It was the

Saturday night that you and Sally got into that big fight. I think that was the same evening that you pulled the knife on her. It was raining, and you sped off in Sally's car. Alisa jumped in my car to chase you. Sally, on the other hand, was trying to run (where to I don't know), and I was on foot chasing her (which wasn't that tough since I was in shape and much taller than she). I can still remember jogging along beside her, saying, "You can't outrun me. Can we just talk about this?"

It was all so dramatic. What a night that was! I guess that was the official beginning of your "great escape." My other memories are of cheesecakes and after-church dinners, the aquarium, the dog, and laughs—lots of laughs . . .

Whew! The flashbacks must have been deep. When I read about it, my heart just broke. I just keep saying, "You just don't know what people are going through." I mean, we were right there and didn't know. Now, years later, we hear that you went through this living hell (of course, to come through shining as pure gold, praise the Lord!).

Anri, know that I am so humbled and honored by your "for such a time as this" comment. Knowing myself, it always amazes me that God uses me anyway! And I thank you for sharing. There are not that many people whom you can have absolutely no communication with for years and then pick up the relationship in a sense closer than you left off. God's timing is perfect. "And it shall come to pass, that before they call, I will answer; and while they are yet speaking, I will hear" (Isa. 65:24, KJV). And you know what really amazes me? That years ago when we met God knew about this particular time in both our lives. He knew that at this point in our lives we would need each other. It is so amazing! Every time I think about it I just want to scream that God is awesome! I am so honored and excited to be a part of the restoration process!

Now, answer these questions for me if you will:

How old were you when the molestation stopped?

What types of decisions did you make regarding "consensual sex" (prior to marriage)?

§ § §

Hello, Gwen. It's a busy day, and I'm preparing to go out of town, so let me get right to your questions. Because I blocked out much of my memory I don't know when the abuse stopped. I remember that when I moved into the big bedroom because all the other girls had gone, I put a lock on my door. Going home from college was never something I wanted to do. Something inside tells me that it stopped when I was about 13, because my menses started about then, but I can't be sure.

Promiscuity was part of my experience. I should say selective promiscuity. Gwen, I was 15 or 16 and men— not young guys—would offer me a ride home. I'd accept, and they'd take me home with them. There I teased and allowed them to "go only so far." It's a wonder someone didn't rape me. Somehow I always escaped by telling them that I was a virgin and 15—jail bait! I got my kicks and then sent them off.

There were many such instances, even during my college years. The guys I was involved with were not students but older men who hung around campus, preying on the younger girls. It was the same game every time. I would say, "Good girls don't go all the way." I deceived myself by telling myself that I was "still a virgin." I recognize now what a lie I believed and how I have hurt others as a result. Sometimes I just wonder how in the world I ever survived to tell about it. I was so hurt, so vulnerable, so ignorant, so stupid, so lonely, so afraid—and so protected by God!

My physical relationship with Sally was basically the same. I know you didn't ask for this, but you will get it anyway. From what I understand (not my experience), homosexuals have oral sex or vaginal penetration with fingers or other objects and anal sex by the same method—penetration. Still clinging to the mind-set that I was a virgin and that no one had "penetrated" me, I wasn't about to let Sally be the first person to do that. So we went through the same scenario again and again, me teasing, seducing, and pretending I wanted what she did, then I would leave her hanging just as I did with the guys not so many years before. Now, I realize that all I wanted was to be loved. It always ended with her being extremely frustrated with me. I figured with her just like I did with the guys that it wasn't real sex. Therefore, God couldn't be that mad at me—after all, we never went "all the way."

I was in serious denial. I understand as I talk with women who have had homosexual relationships that they don't consider it sex because there is no penetration involved. (I guess I'm not the only one who has lived in denial.) To keep Sally from badgering me, I compromised to appease her, but always left feeling dirty, ashamed, and angry. Often I punished her for "making me do that." Sally will tell you to this day that we never had "sex."

The night I drove away in her car was the beginning of the "great escape." By then I was just fed up with the control and anger, and my impulses told me to get out fast. So I did. I was tired of pleading, lying, and trying to act as if I enjoyed being controlled when I actually hated it. I had put up with it only because she met some of my needs, but it was time to go—and go I did. I recognized that I could live without her. I wouldn't die. After all, I was the one making the money and could work anywhere. But it was still very hard to make the decision. Even when I did leave I acted on impulse, not reason. I know now that God used my irrational state of mind to bring me to a rational decision.

(I stopped for a break and considered that some of this stuff I have never talked about. The good news is that I have no shame, just thankfulness to the Lord. You understand?)

Anyway, this is vital. 1 Corinthians 6:16 says in effect that when people join themselves together by intercourse, consensual or forced upon them, a bond forms between the two people. The development of that bond means you are now tied to that person or those persons, male or female, in the most intimate way. When the relationship ends, the tie is still there. Or when you or the other person gets another sexual partner the bond remains. And even when you marry, the bond lingers. It creates problems in the marriage relationship. Skeletons surface that Satan uses to haunt you. They prevent you from experiencing the fullness of the marital relationship. Only prayer and the power of Jesus can break such unholy, unhealthy, sinful bonds. It is best if the prayer is specific and the person asks God to break the sinful bonds with the other person. Also, if the person is married, he or she needs to ask God to help them form healthy and holy bonds with their spouse.

Experience tells me this works. It removed the skeletons from the closet of my heart and mind. After praying, I belonged only to my husband and not to all those other people too. It was a difficult process, but God answers prayer!

Anri

§ § §

Let me tell you that you are really an inspiration to me. You have found such freedom in the Lord, and it is exciting! I am so proud of you and happy that I can call you friend, because of what you have allowed God to do for, with, and through you. You're such an example of what life with Christ is really all about. I have added you to my prayer list, and I ask God that He will continue to use you even beyond your imagination. Also I pray that He will bind Satan (who I know isn't very happy with you).

Anri, I know that on some level talking about all of this can't be easy, even though it is obviously very liberating. So, know that the pattern has been set. I am not going anywhere, and we will continue to explore and question till we are finished.

See ya,
Gwen

Hey, Anri, yeah, it's me again. I got my hair done today and decided to reread the mail that you sent to me. I must say that the second time was even better than the first, and the first was good! But of course, upon the second reading, I have more questions:

Explain a bit about some of the addictions you have had to deal with.

Did your brother abuse your sisters too? Have you had conversations with your father or brother since your recovery began?

What was it like for you when God, in the midst of your

own pain, began to show you how you were wrong? Just a comment: Isn't that just like God to show you your faults while you are in the midst of pointing out the faults of others to Him? God is something else, huh?

Take good care and may God bless your socks off today (and every day!).

Gwen

§ § §

Hi, Gwen, About the addictions . . . What is curious is that I knew I had them after I began the process of recovery, but they weren't very clear to me. They became obvious in an interesting way. Someone asked me to write my story. Naturally, I was nervous and scared. I sat down on the floor and thought about all the things that I could do to make myself feel better. I realized after I made my list that *they* were my addictions. An addiction is anything that you use to divert your attention or provide comfort for the source of your distress. I'd rather eat than face my fears, rather talk to my friends about their problems than face my own, or rather shop than feel the pain of being ignored by my husband. Just as there are extremes in food addictions—for example, the overeater and the anorexic—so also there are extremes in the other addictions, involving either indulgence or avoidance. It is the same thing for work, sex, even church. If it makes me feel better, I'll do it. Doesn't that sound like a drug addict? Same principle, different "drug of choice."

Most people have some type of addiction that they just don't recognize. We can even abuse prayer. When we pray about all manner of things and feel so much better afterward, without addressing the painful and ugly issues of our hearts, we have just "used" God and prayer. God not only calls us to pray, He also expects us to deal with sin in our lives. He gives us the power to overcome sin through Him.

As for the brother who molested me . . . My brother was a rageaholic like my dad, and even though he was about three years younger than I, he still overpowered me and caused me a lot of fear and grief. I was everybody's victim. You could look at me cross-eyed and I would cry or shrink back. Because I never fought back, he took advantage of that.

Generational sin is powerful. My brother is in prison for 50 years for molesting our niece and our cousin. Of course he denies it, just like Dad does. He talks a lot, I understand, about God and religion but denies the truth behind them. I have spoken to my dad about three times on the issue. Basically he denied, and still denies, everything. Once I talked with him in order to free myself, so to speak. I explained to him the extent of the damage he had caused me and that I forgive him. Still he denied everything. But I think the guilt caught him.

Shortly afterward he became very sick. We thought he was going to die, but he bounced back. Today he is paranoid and doesn't leave his house. He thinks the police are after him, that I reported him, and that people are trying to get him. It is really pathetic.

I can tell you that at one point I was so angry that I wanted to kill my dad. Instead, I sentenced him to eternity in hell. God had to begin showing me the truth about myself. He had to reveal to me the truth of Romans 2:1 that says in essence that we should not be quick to judge and that if we do condemn others we are just passing judgment on ourselves. It was the first step He used to bring me to forgiveness. I had to see it or I'd think that I was much better than he. But it was a hard thing, especially the realization that I was doing the same thing as he had done, in essence if not in act. I had to look at my own child and see the pain I had caused as a result of my intense anger and hatred. I still am deeply hurt when I see the extent of the damage I have done, and I pray daily for the restoration and healing of my child. A great kid, yes! But hurt nonetheless. I take responsibility for that.

How could You, God, trust me with a precious bundle of Your love? I wonder. Even though You know my tendency and my vulnerability. I am still awed by such love. I trust His power in me.

§ § §

(Against my better judgment I called Anri. We had been communicating via e-mail for a week or so, and I wanted to hear her voice. The conversation was strained, but because I hadn't spoken to her in so many years, I wasn't sure.)

Anri, am I overanalytical, or did I notice a little tension in your voice when we talked on Friday? In the meantime, I will tell you what I experienced during and after our conversation. First of all, I couldn't believe that you recognized my voice. That really freaked me out. Much deeper than that, though, I feel a sense of sadness. It was as if maybe we (Alisa and I) shouldn't have called. Maybe it wasn't really the right time. Maybe you were ready for only "computer to computer" communication, but not anything beyond that. Maybe you just thought that you had worked through all of this stuff and hearing our voices just brought back too much too soon.

I spent much of Friday afternoon pondering about what

you might be thinking, wondering if what I had heard was real or imagined, asking God to fix anything that I may have messed up and to be with you wherever you were.

It is Sunday, and I started this e-mail on Friday, but decided that I would just hang on to it until I heard from you. However, after talking to Alisa, we decided that we really wanted you to know a few things, so here goes:

1. First and foremost, we love you and are happy to be back in touch with you. To us your past is past. We thank God for your present and your future!

2. This seems like unfinished business in many ways, and we are willing to help you to complete this chapter of your life.

3. We especially wanted you to know that neither of us have lived perfect lives. As a matter of fact, God has had to do His share of cleaning up within us as well. We don't say this to minimize your experience, but to let you know that Satan has had his hand in all of our lives. In some cases we allowed him to be the boss, but now we are living a life of freedom with Christ. Perfect lives, no. Forgiven lives, yes!

Just one other thing. A prayer for you. But you can't read and close your eyes at the same time (smile).

Father, in the name of Jesus I come. First of all, I give You all the praise just because You are Lord; I have thanked You so many times for putting Anri back into my life. Now, I have the opportunity to thank You in her "presence." Thank You, God, for her friendship in the past and our renewed friendship now. Thank You!

You know, Lord, that I am grateful right now that You are God. I am thankful that before we call You answer, and while we are yet speaking You hear. While I am yet struggling for the right words to pray, You already have this thing under control. So, God, I will pray that You will bless

Anri as she remembers, talks about, and writes about an unpleasant part of her history. I ask that as she has already shared some things that You will give her the confidence to know that You are in all this process. Help her not to have the "Oh, I-can't-believe-I-said-that feeling" that often comes after a disclosure of this magnitude.

Lord, help me to be the friend, support, and safe person that You would be pleased with and proud of. You know that already she has been such a blessing to my life and Alisa's life and to countless others. Please bind Satan, as he will use any opportunity, including this interaction, to wreck havoc. Most of all, Lord, I just ask for my friend that You will continue the work that You have begun in her life. And when the time is right, God, we look forward to talking, sharing, and catching up in person. But most of all, God, we want to live with You in a place where the strong do not bully the weak, a place that has no injured people to hurt other people. Above all else, God, that is our desire. If You grant only one part of this prayer, Lord, just save us so that we can be at the best reunion of all— the one that won't require AT&T, Sprint, MCI, or a good airfare. Lord, we just want to stand on that sea of glass with You. Save us, please. In the awesome, amazing, wonderful name of Jesus Christ we pray and give You thanks. Amen!

Anri, I love you.
Gwen

§ § §

Will you answer a question for me, Gwen? When did you know that you had the gift of discernment?

I wish I were alone right now. As I read your e-mail I cried. I wish I could just go and cry and cry. But my family wouldn't understand, and explaining isn't something I want to do right now. I have felt a need to cry most of the day. But now I really want to bawl. Yes, you heard something in my voice. I'm not sure exactly what to call it. After talking to you I stretched out on my bed and recognized the tension that was in my body. Let me try to process this with you, OK?

Somehow, I knew that you would call that day. I don't have caller ID, but I just knew when the phone rang. It was scary. Gwen, I don't remember the last time I saw you. However, I do remember the last time I talked to you on the phone. It was after I left, and I think Sally put you up to calling me to ask me why. Of course, she also wanted you to tell me that I should come back. At least that's what I remember. I also remember you suggesting that I do what I thought was best. I recall your loyalty to both of us.

Please don't think you messed anything up. I don't think I have worked through all the issues of the past. It is difficult unless God in His gentle persistence keeps bringing people up to facilitate my recognition that something is still undone.

I experience uneasiness when I go to large church conferences and run into people that I knew back then. I think I experienced the same feeling when I saw Alisa several years ago. Often I wish I knew what people were thinking. And because I don't, I find I play it cautious until I know I'm safe. You know that safety is about an internal condition, not about whether you, Gwen, are a safe person. It's about my security in Christ, what He says and what He has done for me. I must admit my deep regret for my choices and the shame that still plagues me sometimes. But I choose to believe the truth that "there is therefore now no condemnation to them which are in Christ" (Rom. 8:1, KJV). I choose to reject the lies that the enemy constantly tries to use against me. And I accept God's unconditional love through you, my friend. But sometimes it is hard to accept that. You understand?

Gwen, I have very good friends who know all about me, who cry with me and process with me and fight with me, friends whom I can tell absolutely anything without fear of disclosure or shame, and who hold me accountable. I am accustomed to relating on a deep level with others. But I have never had anyone come into my life at such a deep level as you instantly did! Even in support groups there is a time of testing the waters. I also realize that in most of my relationships I am the one doing the leading.

I have experienced this level of discernment in only one other person. Coupled with the gift of compassion and the desire for honesty, it makes you a rare person with a rare combination of gifts. I see I won't be able to do any hiding here. But I don't mind one bit having my feet held to the fire, so to speak. Please, let God use you fully in this process. Believe me, it will go faster like that.

Thank you for your willingness to go through this "unfinished business" with me. Although I don't think you and Alisa have had spotless lives, I do wonder if you really understand and if in this process I will find that you will really be there for me. I expect some painful days as I work through this stuff; I've already had some as I walk through this valley. But as God promised, I will find a greater revelation of Himself. I'm in this for the long haul. Are you? I know that this process could get pretty depressing. Some people can't deal with that.

You can pray for me anytime. That was/is a powerful prayer. I think I will type it out and put it on my mirror. I can't get past the first sentence without crying.

Gwen, it's not often you find someone rejoicing in you. That's what you have done. Man, that's awesome. And you are rejoicing in the Anri you knew. I can't seem to grab on to that one!

Thanks for letting the King of kings use you. Thanks for being real. And thanks for your love. I think I'll go cry now.

Love you more,
Anri

§ § §

Anri, we are together on this one. I too have wanted to cry and have been looking for a reason all weekend. I guess the easiest thing to do is start at the beginning of your e-mail and just respond to some of the things you brought up.

The gift of discernment. Anri, I don't know about that. Can't say I ever thought of it as discernment. In your case, though, I knew right away that something was wrong. When you said, "Hello, Gwen," it shocked me that you recognized my voice.

Very interesting that you "knew" I was calling. Maybe you are the one with the discerning spirit (or maybe you are psychic, hahaha). As for our last conversation, I remember it only because you mentioned it. Interestingly enough, I was probably hedging, because Sally was there. But even then I had to tell the truth. If you felt like you needed to leave (and that was pretty obvious), then you had to go!

OK, this may be a little rocky, but I'm going to take a stab at articulating this. I should have known that it wasn't quite time for us to talk. All that you have gone through and how God has blessed I compare to a funeral (stick with me). You know how when a person dies and you see a close family member, it makes you feel good that they are doing well, even though you know that they will have tough days ahead? You are just relieved and willing to go with the moment when they talk about how God is sustaining them, etc. When they laugh, you laugh. Or when they want to eat ice cream or watch a dumb movie on TV, you kind of go along, convincing yourself that they really are OK. Well, in a sense, I knew that your healing couldn't be finished in just a few short years. And you did say that God was still working on and in you.

Three things should have stood out for me. (1) I was very excited to share your success. (2) You and I share the tendency to look and act as if we have it all together when in fact that may not be the case. (3) You, of course, wanted me to know that the confused, hurt, and lonely Anri that left in the early 1980s was long gone.

Anri, do you realize that if you were the exact same person today that you were back then, I would still be happy and excited to hear from you? It's true.

The unconditional love thing is deep, and I certainly hope that you will accept it. It's free, and by definition you can't get "good enough" to earn it anyway.

I can't say that I understand, because I haven't gone through your experience, nor am I you. But I can say that as you go through the process I'll be there. I fully recognize that there literally isn't another person who can do this like I can. Not because I have any great talent, but because I was there.

Yes, I'm in it for the long haul. I'll continue to remind you of that. As for it getting depressing, I have to trust God to take care of me. Depression is a low price to pay for the true release and freedom of a dear friend. Anri, I'll spend money, be depressed, shed tears, lose sleep, endure pain . . . whatever, to see you through this process. Generally, I prefer to show instead of tell, but right now it's important to me that you understand as much as possible that I am here. As time goes on my actions will catch up with my words.

Anri, the fact that you need to complete the work means just that. You've started a process that isn't yet finished. I think that people still in the healing process have a level of understanding, sympathy, and empathy that others can't relate to. You are a tremendous witness for God, proof that He finishes what He starts and that He truly moves in the lives of people. We must "grow in grace," and you are doing just that.

Whenever I think of God using me, I shiver. He is such an awesome God, and I am me . . . in need of His grace.

As I sign off I wish that I could just give you a big 'ol hug and we could both get our tears out. I thank you for letting me in, and don't start this "I love you more stuff" with me (smile), because I do love you more!

§ § §

I felt so betrayed and unprotected, because when initially I began to share with you, it wasn't with the expectation that it would show up in a book. I've written my story a couple times, but tonight I read my story. One thing about sexually abused people is that we never, ever want to feel unprotected. We will do anything to keep our secrets, and when we venture to tell the hard, dark things, it is very important that the information be treated with kid gloves.

Reading my story and knowing that others would see it was more than I could take. I didn't want anyone to read that stuff—I just couldn't do it. I couldn't share it. Gwen, I contacted the author of the book and told her not to use my story. But you know, I thought about it and realized that God is a God of yesterday, today, and tomorrow. He loves us in our mess, and nothing can ever change His love. Once we come to accept the power of that love to change, repair, clean up, and restore, it doesn't matter who knows what and who might misunderstand something. All that is important is that I am precious, and God is faithful.

Though you already know it, I just need to tell you again that God is more than wonderful! The locusts of pain and bitterness, the canker worm of isolation and despair, the caterpillar of denial and self-hate, and the palmer worm of confusion had all eaten their way through my soul and spirit. My heart was a waste, a howling wilderness. "But God, who is rich in mercy, because of His great love with which He loved us, even when we were dead in trespasses, made us alive together with Christ" (Eph. 2:4, 5, NKJV). God stepped into the dark cavern called my heart and spoke words of love, power, and healing.

I realize it will take more than one session of sitting at His feet just as it took more than one day to create the earth. But I am confident that He who began my transformation will complete it. God is doing what He promised, Gwen. He is restoring the years destroyed by abuse and pain. God wants *His* story told, Gwen. He wants us to be able to say with Joseph, "Satan meant it for evil but God meant it for good." His story is of victory. His story is of freedom. And His story is of healing and power. Today, I choose to stand as a witness to His character. In all this, God is faithful! Praise Him! (And yes, I told the author she could use my story!)